THE END OF SAN FRANCISCO

THE END OF SAN FRANCISCO

Mattilda Bernstein Sycamore

City Lights • San Francisco

Cover photograph by Florencia Aleman of Brian Goggin's artwork: "Defenestration," located at the corner of 6th & Howard Streets, San Francisco, CA, 1997 – present.

Cover deisgn by em dash

Although this is a work of nonfiction, many names have been changed.

Library of Congress Cataloging-in-Publication Data
Sycamore, Mattilda Bernstein.
The end of San Francisco / Mattilda Bernstein Sycamore.
    pages cm
    ISBN 978-0-87286-572-3
1. Sycamore, Mattilda Bernstein. 2. Lesbians—United States—Biography.
3. Lesbians—United States—Identity. 4. Gays—United States. I. Title.

HQ75.4.S93A3 2012
306.76'63092—dc23
[B]

                    2012046897

City Lights Books are published at the City Lights Bookstore
261 Columbus Avenue, San Francisco, CA 94133
www.citylights.com

To Andy Slaght, for always believing in me (once more with feeling!)—and, for telling me to leave (even if I didn't listen) . . .

For JoAnne, 1974-1995
For Chrissie Contagious, 1974-2010
For David Wojnarowicz, 1954-1992

CONTENTS

THE FIRST TIME

I don't know what's possible, as my mother and I drive through pitch-dark suburbs that I barely recognize until we get right near the house—were those same lights always at the end of the driveway? The trees are even bigger than I remember, driveway cracked in even more places. The kitchen has discarded that '70s greenish yellow for cobalt blue cabinets with sleek white counters and illuminated glass tiles. I can't go past the kitchen, to that bed in the family room where my sister sits with her boyfriend and the attendant, talking to my father. I walk around the other way, through the living room with the marble café table that I treasured as a teenager because it reminded me of New York, next to the piano and a newer Persian rug with a smaller, more elegant sofa. The hallways look brighter, wood floors almost pulsating—the paintings glow. Only the bathroom is identical—pink and green tiles, green tub and toilet, chrome towel holders—now it almost looks vintage.

Back in the front of the house, my sister and her boyfriend come into the kitchen to hug hello and then I'm accidentally looking right at my father, so I go into the family room to stand there kind of frozen with my hand on my right hip—I can see myself seeing him, looking at him like I'm daring everything. The attendant looks tense. My sister isn't breathing, her boyfriend looking up then down. My father opens his eyes, closes them. Opens them, closes them. After it's clear that he's not going to say anything, I sit down on a leather recliner with a wooden pedestal, an updated version of the one they used to have. It's actually comfortable.

They've painted the knotted pine walls a gray color that my grandmother always called putty, the color she saw as the neutral-yet-sophisticated answer to too much white. Everything looks more contemporary, the ceilings higher and I realize it's because they've replaced the track lighting with recessed lighting. I'm studying my father, gray hair receding but not as much as it could be, considering his age and condition. He has the same pillow as I do—the extra-soft foam one my mother found—his even has a black pillowcase like the one I borrowed from a friend. Every now and then, my father gets agitated and his hands move around like they're part of a different person, and my sister asks: Are you okay? Do you need something to drink?

My sister, her boyfriend, and the attendant are watching *Survivor* and I glance over to glimpse various almost-naked athletic male bodies and women in bikinis—someone just lost something, and I guess people like this show because it's like porn. Then my sister switches the station and it's *Deal or No Deal*, she says have you seen this? A bald-headed guy with a diamond earring says something and then twenty or thirty model-type women in identical blue dresses and heels give serious synchronized runway while carrying silver metal briefcases down a flight of stairs and the announcer says Hi ladies. Hi Howie, they all say at the same time, modeling pin-up compliance for a new generation. My sister tells me how some show about end-of-life issues came on earlier and she didn't know whether to change the channel. She didn't want to be too obvious, even though they were talking about pulling the plug, so she decided to leave the show on. As if on cue, a bald woman flashes on screen, something about how cancer is beautiful.

My mother comes in and brushes my father's hair back with her hand, a gesture of intimacy I've never seen before. Then she's standing at the foot of the bed rubbing his legs, and his hands start moving around again, his face looks pained and my sister says what are you doing? He likes this, my mother says—I'm massaging his legs to stimulate him. Then she says: Matthew's here. And he looks around more animated: Oh hi Matthew, how are you?

I don't know if I start crying right then or if it's later, but really everything is crying, I'm sobbing softly then loudly then softly again, another burst and then my mother comes over as if to comfort me, I say please don't touch me, she goes back to the other side of the room. Later, somewhere in this sobbing, my sister comes over too and I hold her hands and say thank you, but please don't touch me.

If I'm trying to establish a narrative here, crying is that narrative and everything else is around it. *Elemental* is the word I'm thinking of—crying is elemental, the rest is important too but I can't reestablish the order with all this crying. I say what did you think of my letter? He looks confused: I don't think I read it. Would you like me to read it to you now? Yes.

Can I say something about my father's voice? Feeble is not the word I would use, though I can see others invoking it. Can

I possibly choose innocent? Softer and almost childlike. I say to my mother: Could you get the letter?

My mother, standing at the head of the bed, eyes squinting from panicked determination: That is not possible.

Me, standing at the foot of the bed: Karla thinks I'm going to give you a stroke.

My mother: There are other things to talk about besides the letter.

Is this when I start sobbing? It makes more sense here, if here is about sense. This is the moment made for the movies, I can feel my chest arching forward, head back—this is the fight-or-flight reflex, I mean the fight part. I say: You're just trying to control his death because you couldn't control your life with him. And the tears pouring down my face are like armor—I'm cold in the the way I learned to survive as a kid except now I'm also crying, it's both at the same time and my father says: Is that true, Karla?

The attendant is the first one to excuse herself from the room and then my sister's boyfriend, and then my sister asks if I'd like her to leave, yes, and eventually my mother leaves too but I can hear both of them lurking in different places, trying not to make any noise. I want to say that the words aren't important it's the feeling that matters, except the words are important and the feeling matters. I'm crying and my father's crying and are we crying together?

But what are the words? I'm trying to re-create the letter, saying: When I first heard that you had cancer, it surprised me because even though for so long I'd wanted any trace of you to disappear from my life, I found myself wishing that I could save you. I started thinking about different health care modalities I could suggest—acupuncture, guided visualization, meditation. I realized I still had some hope that you'd come to terms with sexually abusing me, that you would acknowledge it and then we could have some mundane conversation about publishers or something else from my life I thought you might be interested in.

I see his face tense up into a grimace when I say sexually abuse, but where I'm really crying, probably the most except for at the beginning, is when I say: I wish you could acknowledge sexually abusing me, because it would make it easier for me to go on living. I'm asking for something that he could give me. He's crying too, a few tears dripping down his face and he says thank you for sharing your letter. And then there are so many layers to my sobbing: there's holding the chest while spasming anyway; there's tears gliding smoothly down skin; there's tears in eyes, in face, inside everything.

What I want to do is to touch his arm, softly, his skin. It feels intimate and nurturing and dangerous, and right now I'm okay with all these sensations. I tell him I've learned there are other ways to be strong besides holding everything in—and of course here there is more sobbing—sobbing is the texture of the air, sobbing is the feeling of this room, sobbing here it feels like strength.

At some point he's choking and I ask if he's okay and then my sister magically appears to ask if he needs anything to drink. My father looks confused, holds his hand up and it swings in the air. Can you get something for Matthew, he says? Allison asks him if he wants ginger ale. I ask for a bottle of water, if there's one that's warm, and Allison returns with a glass of ginger ale and the water. My father pushes away the ginger ale—Matthew, he says. Oh, I have water, I say. My father pushes the ginger ale away again, Allison says I'll just leave it here for you.

Did I mention that I can see my mother standing in the

doorway of the dining room, eyes narrowed while drinking a beer, and at this point she emerges with the postcard for my new book in her hand, that's what she wants me to talk about. I hand it to him—at this point, why not? He reads the title, or part of it—I can't tell which part—I think he says he likes the cover. I ask if he wants me to read the blurb, since the print is so small and he's having difficulty seeing, although then I'm not sure if he understands what I'm reading. At this point I'm talking softly—I can't tell if it's because of intimacy or because everyone's listening—I think they've moved farther away, but I'm not sure.

There are moments of silence and then there are points where I'm talking about more distant topics, even though I'm not sure if I should, since it's not like my father has acknowledged anything. I'm describing the gentrification in the neighborhood where he and my mother are buying a condo, the displacement to make way for richer people's leisure activities. At one point he says something that I don't understand, it sounds like: You're a very compelling liar. But he doesn't look like that's what he's saying. I ask him to repeat himself but he doesn't—talking is difficult for him, a lot of the time we're together his eyes are closed and I ask if he's tired, he says no. I say is it because of the drugs, and he doesn't say anything. I say your eyes are closed, but you're listening, right? He nods. This might be the first time he's ever listened to me.

At one point there's a single tear dripping down his cheek—I touch it with my finger, then brush his hand softly. It feels almost sexual in this moment, even if it's scary to acknowledge that. My mother enters the kitchen to ask the attendant if it's time to give my father his meds—the attendant asks him if that's what he wants, and he tightens his face and hands, not yet. Even though earlier his whole body became one large spasm, fighting the pain, and I asked if he needed anything. I didn't expect to want to care for him.

I tell my father I'm leaving, it's time for them to give him his medication—or at least that's what they think, what the doctors think, even though the medication takes away his ability to express himself clearly. Though it's hard to tell what's the medication and what's cancer. I say I'm glad that you asked me to share the letter, he says I'm glad too. He says will you be here when I wake up? I say no, but I will come back tomorrow night.

When I leave the room, I don't feel afraid of the house anymore, I can go downstairs where so much of everything happened. His office looks much cleaner, the carpet newer—no stains of mold or come, images of the past or even fear really. The door to the rec room is scarier, especially when I can't find the light right away, but even behind the bar, in that moldy sink where I was a broken toy—I don't know, it's harder to feel all that while also feeling everything now. Like the chimney where I'd imagine myself floating away, away from him splitting me open, right now it just looks like a chimney.

On the toilet in the downstairs bathroom are seashells that I arranged fifteen years ago: I used to like decorating the bathrooms. The shells are actually beautiful, furrowed green and mother-of-pearl swirls, I put one in my pocket. The dark closet we called the wine room is the eeriest, the floor tiles crumbling and mold exposed, but the basement looks clear of most of the mold: the tiles have been removed, and the cement floor painted tan. I wonder where they moved all of my grandmother's paintings that they use to store here, the ones they didn't like. The refrigerator with an icemaker that I battled my father to get—a teenage consumer victory—it's now in the basement, outdated, holding bottled water and sodas.

Back upstairs, in the room where I used to sleep—I'm

resisting calling it my room, like everyone else calls it—the bed is the same, the comforter from before, the same gray walls. A gray I chose, different from my grandmother's putty. Then there's the black lacquered desk I got at IKEA when it first opened, the display case with the minerals my grandmother gave me, a glass panda on the bookshelf, a clay bird, wooden eggs. I didn't expect these things to feel comforting, but I actually want to take some of them home. Especially when I discover the stuffed animals still in the drawer underneath the bed—all the mice who were my friends, even the little pigs I'd forgotten about—all arranged just as I'd left them.

In my sister's room, she and her boyfriend are lying on the bed and I join them. My sister asks how I'm doing. I can't tell how you're feeling, she says, you hold everything in. She's the one who's holding everything in—I resent her so much more in this house, holding on to my father as if he gave her what she needed.

My sister shows me another of my stuffed animals—Henry the hippo—she has him in her room. He's much larger than the rest and I hold him: I ask my sister to take a picture, back in my room on the bed. I'm smiling like a little kid—this is when I love her and then my mother comes in to show me a protest sign I made that she's kept in the closet, from the first Gulf War. Isn't that so perceptive, she says.

Suddenly my mother's in nurturing mode. She says she'll send me anything I want, these are my things, of course I should have them. Do you want to stay here tonight, she says—I think you'd like the Spring Air mattress. The mattress she and my father were sleeping on, because he couldn't sleep in their bed—I saw it leaning against the wall in the living room, and it did look kind of comfortable. But I'm not staying here, even if it feels okay right now. So we're gathering things to bring back to my father's office, the apartment where sometimes I slept on drunken teenage nights, missing some essentials—pillows, sheets, plates, a glass, fork, knife, spoon. I snap a few photos of the backyard in pitch dark, though the camera I bought at the drugstore doesn't do anything wide-angle enough to capture the trees.

I dream about the Holocaust like I used to as a kid, except that back then I always woke up just as I was about to die—this time, I escape into Sweden with my mother, she says we're Swedish and I wake up as they're about to let us in. I'm trying to appreciate the symbolism, but it's way too early in the morning and I feel horrible, my whole body imprisoned by that fibromyalgia ache, sinuses twisted. I make it up to the roof to sit on the sundeck, huge and empty with only a few plastic chairs although at least they don't hurt my body like metal chairs would. I'm staring at the sun, then out at all the fall trees and no skyline because none of the buildings in DC are allowed to be taller than the Capitol. It's freezing, but the air is so fresh, fall air—this is my moment, and then I crash into another exhausting day.

On the phone, my mother's talking about whether she wants to move into the condo, she says when I bought it I never dreamed I'd be living in it—there's a whirlwind of changes in my life and I don't know if I'm ready. Then Allison says: It's so hard to see him like this, I don't want him to be in pain—I feel like he's a little bird, and I need to protect him from everything. This morning I handed him a bagel and he was holding it like a napkin, he wanted to spit in it. I think last night he said it was nice to see you, Matthew, and I felt like you were connecting and it broke my heart.

I can't help thinking that when Allison says she wants to protect my father from everything, she means from me. But then we're talking about his death, she says she wants it to be peaceful, and I'm wondering how people usually die from this type of cancer. She says: Sometimes your body organs fail and your mind fills with toxins—or you get pneumonia—or seizures.

So much pain from sleeping on my side—the body pillow doesn't help on this hard mattress. I go on a walk, but what a horrible decision—I turn the corner and there's some sort of new strip mall-type thing on Wisconsin. It's almost hard to believe how posh the stores are: Tiffany, Jimmy Choo, Louis Vuitton, Gucci, Bulgari, Max Mara, Dior, Barneys Coop, Cartier, Ralph Lauren. Down the street, I attempt to tour the bathrooms where I used to cruise, on the way from high school to my father's office: one is gone and the other now looks like a bathroom you'd buy in a box from Home Depot. No more old-fashioned urinals or teal stalls—even the gorgeous old tiled floor has been replaced with shiny granite. And I don't even want to talk about all the security guards roaming the halls in uniform, looking for action. There's even a security desk.

But can I really be upset that Mazza Gallery, the shopping mall with Neiman Marcus where I used to follow and later direct men into the upstairs bathroom, the parking lot, the underground stairwell—that formerly posh mall has lost its atrium to make way for an AMC theater? I'm so hypoglycemic that I've made my way to Giant, in back of the faux-Fifth-Avenue mini mall, a brand new grocery store with mountains of potato salad stacked in small, medium, and large plastic containers. Is this what the people who shop at those stores eat?

In DC, people look at me like I'm from another planet—their eyes open wide or they start pointing, or their mouths just hang open, or they look up and then down and then up and then down. My mother's talking about how my father leaned over to her and said: There was an announcement about satellite forces on TV. She said: I haven't heard anything about that yet. But his colleague didn't know how to act, she says—I had to shake my head a few times at inappropriate things he said. You're not the only one I try to control, though it's a good thing you're here now because I think there will be more changes.

By changes my mother means dementia, then death. She decides not to pick me up because she needs to talk to the new aide when she arrives, so I take a cab with a driver who won't speak to me. I assume it's because I'm a faggot. I ask him to turn the heat down; he turns it up. Why do I tip him anyway?

Back at the house, Allison has just microwaved popcorn and my mother says don't you like the smell of it? I don't. Allison says do you want some? My mother says no, I just ate half a piece of chocolate cake. Allison comes into the dining room and puts three pieces of candy on the table: a sour ball, two Now and Laters. My mother goes googly-eyed, looks back at her bills.

In the family room, my father's yelling for Helen, the attendant, in a dry, demanding way while Helen asks are you in pain, Mr. Bill, are you in pain? And already I'm afraid again. My mother says: I'm sorry you have to see him this way. I'm sorry I have to see him. I look at the postage stamps on the dining room table, shades of blue and purple with yellow handwriting. I look closer—the writing says STOP FAMILY VIOLENCE.

My mother says did you use everything in that package I got you from Bloomingdale's? She means the bedding and the towels that were waiting at my father's office when I arrived. I shouldn't even answer, but instead I say I used the sheets, but I didn't wash them. I used the quilt, but I left the tag on it so you can still return it. How much was the quilt, my mother says.

I wonder if it was the explosion with my mother last time

that helped to dispel my fear. My mother says do you want to go on a walk around the house while he's getting ready? I line up all my old stuffed animals on the bed where I used to sleep, an extended family. My mother says: I'd be afraid if I saw that one out on the street. My sister says: I guess you liked mice. My mother says anything you'd like me to send you, just let me know, and I spot one of the minerals my grandmother gave me in the dining room—dioptase, a sparkling emerald green that was my favorite jewel. I ask about the small piece of art by Roy Liechtenstein, discreetly hanging in the hallway, an abstract unlike his famous cartoons, it's just the background—I used to stare at the 3-D games it plays, my eyes going somewhere. My mother says: I'll think about that.

Downstairs are all these reports I wrote from fourth to sixth grade, or maybe even earlier—each one has a colorful cover decorated with Magic Marker designs and illustrations: Marco Polo; Artemis; The Countries of Central America; Washington, DC History; Six Tales of Nuliajuk; the Federal Republic of Nigeria; Stalin's Russia; Mrs. Frisby; and the Rats of NIMH. I used to get so excited about each assignment—I don't see my report on the Mormon temple, but that's the one I remember the best because I took photos from the front but you couldn't go inside unless you were Mormon. They would only let you go to the visitors' center, where they tried to convert you. My mother says she wants to keep the reports, but she'll make me copies. In my father's files, there's an autobiography he started to write while doing his psychiatric residency in New York—it mentions that he grew up living with his grandparents and his uncle, as well as his parents. I don't know much about my parents' history—they weren't interested in sharing it.

Back in the dining room, my mother says: Dad's asleep because he was in a lot of pain, do you want to come back tomorrow? I don't want to come back tomorrow, but I say that's okay. I go into the room with the computer—that same room I could still call mine if I wanted to. I hook up my laptop to the DSL cable, so I can use the voice activation software. My mother comes in every five minutes and fucks up what I'm typing—are you ready? When I'm sort of done, I go into my mother's room—she and my sister are lying on the bed in opposite corners, chatting—they look kind of cute and I start to sit in between them but then I'm not sure if that's what I want, so I sit on the sofa.

My mother and I are getting ready to leave; I go into the family room to say goodbye to Helen and there's my father sitting straight up, staring right at me. It startles me and I ask him how he's doing, he swings his hands in the air like how could I be doing? I tell my mother he's awake, I'll talk to him now, and I ask Helen to leave the room. My mother asks her to stay in the kitchen, but she goes in the living room, and my mother says oh, okay, then comes into the family room to ask if I want her to drive me home. I say I can take a cab, that's no problem. Do you want me to call you one? No, I would like to talk first—could you please leave?

Then I'm talking so quietly, I feel like a child. I ask: Have you thought about our conversation? My father's answer: No. But you remember it, right? He nods his head.

I figure I might as well say what I want and get it over with, so I start: I wish you made different choices after I confronted you about sexually abusing me. You're a psychiatrist—you could have done so much to come to terms with it. Instead you went to someone who specialized in false memory syndrome, and he gathered the whole family together to figure out how to convince me I was wrong.

I talk for a while and whenever my father looks over, his

eyes look sad and huge and I think about how scared I used to be of those same eyes but now it's not overwhelming: I stare right in; he looks away. I say I'm much more nervous tonight, and right then my mother comes back in the room: Are you ready to go?

No, why don't you go to bed? I can take a taxi.

I can't go to bed until I know you're safe.

She goes back into the dining room, loudly opening her bills. I say can you please go into your bedroom? Why can't she just leave us alone, I say to my father. What is she afraid of? I think maybe she's just as invested in your denial as you are. You know—one of the things you've actually been successful at doing is saving a ton of money so she doesn't have to worry about anything, but you've created this false sense of emergency for so long and now she doesn't even understand that you have money. I wish you would just tell her that. He looks at me. I say: Can you tell her that?

I feel fumbling and stupid and inarticulate. I'm not even sure what he can say any more, these moments with me might be his most engaged. I say it's still so hard for me because I locked everything in my body—it hurts to carry a bag, to type, to walk for more than a few blocks, to sleep the wrong way. And then I say what I'm thinking but I'm not sure that I want to say but then I decide to say it anyway: Even though you've caused me more harm than anyone else in my life, I still love you and I don't want you to die and I wish we could have a relationship. And right after love is finally where I'm sobbing, not as loud as last time but with as much intensity. I'm looking right at him so he can see it all. He closes his eyes and I keep staring in his direction.

After a few minutes, my father starts to grimace and I ask: Are you in pain? Then my mother comes in: Does he need something? My father pushes his hands out in exasperation like he wants my mother away and she says oh, okay, I'll leave, and goes back into the other room. Do you have anything to say to me, I ask my father. He shakes his head no, and then I'm sitting there focusing on my breath while looking at his closed eyes. With his head tilted slightly down I can see that the hair is gone in the back: His face looks so long, long but still tan— he must have started out incredibly tan, since I'm sure he hasn't been out in the sun in weeks. He always did sit out a lot in the summer.

I touch his hand and he opens his eyes, a tear clinging to the outside of the eye closest to me. I say: I don't know if I'll see you again, so if there's anything you want to tell me, you can tell me now or you can also ask Karla or Allison to bring the phone. I wonder whether, if he said something about sexually abusing me, they would even tell me.

I want to ask if he's afraid of death, but instead I say: Is there anything you want that you don't have? He shakes his head no, and that's when my mother comes back in and he gets angry, flailing his arms. My mother calls for Helen: Do you think we should give him more medication? Helen says: We have to ask him, he has to say yes. He shakes his head no, clasping his hands together. I say to my mother: You don't need to be here—she looks at me and says you're right, then to him she says: Should I leave? No, he almost yells. Then Helen's moving my father around on the bed, trying to adjust him so he's comfortable. I'm pushing the buttons so the bed leans up and then down, I'm not sure why I'm helping. My father's trying to pull his body up by grasping the bars on the side of the bed and Helen adjusts them so they're higher, she says we don't want you falling off the bed, Mr. Bill. My father looks out at me and my mother: Who is that, he says. I say this is Matthew,

I'm still here. He looks satisfied. Helen says that is Karla, and my father looks at my mother.

Then it's just my father, my mother, and me. My father keeps saying CLOSER, CLOSER—in that dry angry voice, and my mother looks like a little kid inching toward me, her leg brushing against mine, and I think of moving away. My father's trying to pull himself up, maybe so we can all sit on the sofa like a family is what I'm wondering. But he's also grabbing his dick through the hospital gown. We can't fit in bed with you, I say, and he seems to understand. My mother quietly leaves the room.

Then my father looks at the watch on his wrist like he's trying to read the time, except he's looking at the watch band. I turn the watch around and he stares at it. I say do you want me to tell you the time? He nods his head. It's 12:30 a.m. Then he looks me in the eyes and says: Can you help me get up? I say no, I can't help you. He asks: Because of your weakness?

That's when I could get angry, but I decide to save it. I tell him I can adjust the bed, and then I'm pushing the buttons until it's clear that he won't be satisfied with anything, just like before. I can get up, he says, with a very confused and sad look in his eyes like he's already leaving this world, or this room with me anyway. Anyway, I say, I want to say goodbye. He closes his eyes. I love you, I say, and kiss him on the forehead. Still he says nothing.

When I leave the room, I feel calm and light, like I've said everything and I don't need to get dragged into nostalgia for something I never had, to watch my father die and hold his hand. I can hear my mother telling him I'll be back tomorrow—don't promise him that, I say, and she says: Oh.

Backing up in the driveway, I hear the wheels of my mother's car in the grass and I say Karla, the car is slipping off the driveway. She says I know. Then the car starts to scratch against the brick base of one of the lampposts and she says oh, you were right.

The roads are so quiet. It's way past my mother's bedtime and I'm studying the streets for familiarity. We get to River Road, the same route we used to take on the way to school, and I see a small deer bound into the road—stop, I say, STOP. My mother swerves but almost not enough, I'm thinking that hitting a deer would be a terrible terrible way for this night to end. I spot another deer on the opposite side of the road, killed by an earlier vehicle, and a police car is stopped in front of it. My mother says what is a deer doing on River Road? I say it's because there are all these houses, there's nowhere left to go.

TOGETHER

In one of my early club moments, I got inspired by a pounding beat I hadn't heard before to climb up onto a black
dance cube in the red, green, yellow, blue spotlights and
that's where I first heard the deep droning voice in the song
that went "People are still having sex. Lust keeps on lurking . . .
Nothing makes them stop. This AIDS thing's not working."
This was high school, often in the evening I was having sex
with men in public bathrooms but I didn't call it that, it was
a secret world, at the clubs I just wanted to smoke pot and
drink cocktails and dance—I needed to get away from everything that's what dancing was about. It wasn't true that "All the
denouncement had absolutely no effect," but I could pretend
when the floor was shaking with the bass.

That was back when you knew the drug dealer was the
one with the bleached white hair and the lunchbox with smi-
ley-face stickers on it, you didn't really have to hide your drugs

yet, not even in DC, and I could just go crazy on the dance floor it was my space my place to go crazy I needed that. At the beach with my sister I played something by New Order from *Technique* I was showing off all my dance moves I mean I didn't have special moves I would just go with it. My sister looked at me like I was crazy, I said that's how people dance at clubs. And then we went out on the balcony with the boombox echoing off the cement leading out to the ocean and we danced for the echo, for the cement, for the other balconies, probably not for the ocean as much because by the time we remembered the ocean we were just dancing.

Later, after I got away, there was Cajmere's "Brighter Days" with that track clack bringing you right into the vocal hold and then back to clack track but always building. By this point it was all about something clanky, something banging, give me some horns but mostly just that pounding bass layering drums repeating sample layering bass pounding drums yes yes please more yes. Screaming when the beat got knock-you-down overwhelming and breathe-deep soothing at the same time or that sample came at the exact moment when you couldn't possibly handle it or just because you saw the wrong person at the right time or the right person at the wrong time or because there was something missing I mean there was nothing missing for just that moment with the sweat pouring down your face your eyes bringing the beat into your body your body taking it.

So I'm starting conversations with everyone on the way home or at least saying hi and waving. They advertised minimal techno but then it was that beat throwing me into stumbling grace, the way you watch people's moves and build into and away from collapse like anything is possible and then at the end when that guy came up and said thanks for dancing with me. A straight guy doing the raver jock thing oh that was so sweet I mean I wasn't exactly dancing with him except that I'm aware of the bodies in the room and how we interact until I'm not aware of anything except this breath.

But the endorphins, like I'm asleep and awake at the same time because of all the sensation in and under my skin. Then it's the next day, and I'm sitting outside the movie theater because I can't figure out how to sit inside without too much pain— I've tried moving around and even getting up to stretch, then taking off my shoes because my feet feel swollen, then even my socks because it feels too humid and stuffy in the theater. Then someone gets the person working there to tell me I can't eat the food I brought, so I go outside and stare at literally hundreds or maybe thousands of ants crawling up six metal water fountains on the edge of what looks like a miniature sports field. It's art, or near art anyway, and in four of the water fountains there's pigeon shit in carefully delivered rows.

I think about eating while sitting on the toilet because the bathroom has a better cooling system than the theater anyway, but then the same employee who told me not to eat in the theater follows me into the bathroom—I'm guessing there's no rule prohibiting me from eating in the privacy of a bath-room stall, but I feel strange and conspicuous so I go back out-side. I'm sitting on the steps, but then there's so much burning around my neck and down my shoulders so I decide to stand up. Although I don't want to eat standing up so then I sit down again and Derek comes out, he says oh you're eating—I was just checking to make sure you're okay.

He goes back inside, and then I start crying because I'm not okay, I'm really not: I hate that doing something so simple as dancing brings me here to all this pain. The way the beat bends forward and back, hands up into flip twist around the floor just another platform, hands into hands so many hands into bodies another floor around bodies into eyes stretching eyes stretching light into air. And yes, this song where the light is purple, green, red winding out of the dark into all these bodies, me, on the dance floor, and I wake up thinking I should start a club except wait, I can't even dance for more than seven minutes in my house without hurting myself, sometimes even the seven minutes hurts, I mean it usually hurts something. I can't decide whether it's better to do it anyway.

I'm telling Derek about how I get nervous when I decide to go out. Like yesterday I paced back and forth across the street from this one scenester bar, but there were too many people smoking outside—I couldn't deal with walking through the crowd and what if someone wanted to talk to me, then I'd be standing in the middle of all that smoke. But sometimes I get nervous about just the idea of going out and then I keep rushing to the bathroom to shit. Or I'll get to the door of some club and I'll get that sinking stomach drama, well that's always happened but there used to be more of a chance that once I got inside I could walk into the music making my eyes close and it would send me to the sky.

Tonight I'm thinking of going to this disco revival night, even though I hate disco, mostly because it's taking place in the basement of 1015 Folsom and years ago I went to a club in that basement every Tuesday, it wasn't like the rest of the club all fancy just a basement finished in a kind of unfinished way, with a low ceiling like maybe you'd hit your head on the pipes if you jumped too high, and everyone would dance like crazy. It was a Tuesday night so we were dedicated and I'd always get that calm rush from dancing except I remember standing outside at 4:00 a.m. after they closed and all these people were getting into fancy cars and I was trying to find a ride, no one would give me a ride. The club was called Together.

Then, just a few months ago, this guy on the bus asked me if I went out to clubs a lot, I used to, then it turned out he remembered me from Together—he started going on and on about how it used to be all about the dancing you could be anybody and just dance it didn't matter whether you were straight or gay, who you knew or what you looked like, what kind of clothes you wore it was all about the dancing. And if I let my eyelids flutter a bit I can remember him too he used to spin around and jump up and down he was a straight guy who wasn't afraid.

But then there's that certain kind of nostalgia so specific to club life, like you can take any horrible place and suddenly it was the place where everyone got along when the drugs were great when there were no drugs when the drugs were actually fun when everyone was different when everyone was the same before the straight people the yuppies the suburbanites the tweakers the tourists took it over when the music actually built it hit you over the head it was soothing it knocked you down it was all about the vibe when the DJs actually knew how to spin when two hours was a warm-up not a whole set when DJs would play for the music not for the crowd when DJs would actually play for the crowd when DJs would actually spin records when people would actually make out when everyone wasn't just interested in sex when there wasn't so much attitude when there were freaks when there was attitude when people were interesting when people actually had sex when the music was actually good when it wasn't about who you knew when everything was cheap when everything wasn't tacky when you knew everyone when people actually dressed up when everyone wasn't so dressed up when you could have a conversation when the music wasn't so loud when clubs actually had good sound when people would stand in line when there wasn't a line around the block when they didn't frisk you when things were safer when everyone wasn't worried about safety when people would talk to one another when people had fun when everyone got along.

But anyway I'm thinking of going to this disco revival night, even though I hate disco I like that it's in the basement of 1015, which I've just heard was originally one of the big bathhouses in the '70s, so I'd like to look for evidence, maybe those pipes. Plus, there probably won't be smoke, 1015's a big club with too much to lose, they wouldn't risk letting people smoke. A big club with only a few doors that seal like a fortress and this night is in the basement so there's no way for everyone's smoke from outside to get in. And even though I hate disco, I've heard these DJs can actually spin.

But I was talking about my nerves, so of course I'm not there yet. Derek wants to know why I get so nervous, so I think about it and it's strange because either I can't engage and I end up feeling claustrophobic, or I get too excited and then as soon as I'm out of the public eye I can't function I'm just my own head caved in. I wish there was another option—Kid Koala's on now, and when Derek goes to the bathroom I try a few moves and when he comes back out he's looking at me with a mixture of excitement and sadness. I'm sad too because even a few spins and twirls the look in my eyes it's that space I miss the head side to side hands flinging I mean I'm feeling it. And then, just when I'm about to joke that I'll probably hurt something just from these few moves, I notice a pain in my side I don't want to say anything because it'll make me feel hopeless.

I was wrong about the music it was great. I was wrong about 1015 because everybody was smoking I mean everybody it was like no one had ever passed a law. I'm not in favor of the legal system but smoking destroys me. I wish other people would realize that, not about me just about other people but they refuse to. There's plenty of room outside to smoke but no it was inside, everybody was smoking with excitement like they were committing an incredibly transgressive act. Years ago I used to smoke and maybe I smoked that way too. I was wrong because I stayed I mean I knew people were smoking right away there was no way not to know but I couldn't turn around. I mean I didn't.

The place was beautiful—they'd remodeled it so it's a circle with booths on the sides no pipes on the ceiling now there are little lights hanging down, hundreds of them almost like glow sticks in different colors, somehow it looks elegant and everything shimmers and almost the whole place is the dance floor in the center. I even loved the music when the beats got layered like house or dissonant like broken electro except it was disco don't get me wrong I know where house came from. People were festive on the dance floor, sure the '70s look was everywhere but it was more styled than usual and it's sad that the only way queeniness trumps masculinity is when it's high fashion damage, but I'll take damage over masculinity any day.

Maybe I could have left if I hadn't been so surprised—I was surprised by the space it was gorgeous like a cabaret but bigger like a crazed spaceship landing pad. I was surprised that I loved it, even with all the smoking I wanted to dance and once I started dancing I was there. On the dance floor everyone was sweat-drenched letting go I even knew some of the crazier ones and I liked that. I remembered how much I can love clubs all that concentrated energy like you're in a different world where you can watch people watching people watch me I love looking in their eyes and dancing slow and close and fast and far and faster and closer and smiling everywhere and I knew I was wrong.

Dany was working these beautiful queeny dance moves somewhere between vogueing and disco diva and '90s clubkid she was in white, white in the white room so much sweat it was fun to sweat and shake then John who said I haven't seen you in a while and we hugged in all that sweat. I kept thinking I should go before I get tired but really I didn't get tired I just kept dancing or sometimes walking a little and trying to find the air but there wasn't much air. Running into people and then dancing again, this one boy with scenester stubble who was maybe the hottest in the room for me I mean in the sexual way those big eyes he kept staring right at me and I stared back but I was wrong. I wasn't wrong for staring. I wasn't wrong because I didn't get closer to him, I mean maybe I should have gotten closer but I was feeling that place of everywhere at once with my body moving into calculated collapse using falling to find falling apart I mean I am falling apart but not now this is what it means to dance.

I was working the sweater Steven sent me from a thrift store in LA, this gorgeous old sequined wool sweater, sequins in blue yellow purple magenta green teal diamond shapes. I hadn't found the right event for it because wool's usually too warm for me I mean too warm for a layer I don't take off. To-night was the night for this sweater because it was cold out really cold for San Francisco and I figured it would be cold at 1015 too. I almost turned a whole clashing outfit with a torn part of a prom dress around my neck but decided on the pale green corduroys and sparkly purple belt I made the right choice. Even though I was wrong, I made the right choice about my outfit. I felt like I was sparkling too. I mean I was sparkling, but I should've taken one look around and walked right back out-side into the fresh air, the drizzle everyone's complaining about oh the air felt so fresh but I couldn't turn around.

THE TEXTURE OF THE AIR

Sure, here I am again walking through the artificially dark halls of men madly projecting masculinity at any cost because that's what gets them action. But the point is that it no longer matters: suddenly I'm so present. It doesn't make sense really, but I'm laughing and grabbing guys to kiss them on the neck, then I'm devouring this one guy's ear, tongue tasting the hills and valleys and he's hugging me or maybe I'm mostly hugging him but whatever it feels good and starts a trend because then there's the guy with his head nestled at my chin, the few words we exchange are not exactly going anywhere that resembles connection but that's okay too or no, it's not okay, but it's okay.

You can really hear me gulping then the guy's jerking again, then back to my mouth, throat muscles and everything it's like this is the only thing I want to do for the rest of my life. In the hallway, there's an influx of guests because it's almost

35

2:00 a.m., a group of three guys who look younger and trendier than the usual and I'm cruising the one with a bald head and pegged jeans but I think he's intimidated because of his friends. Then there's a tweaker who's a regular, he's kind of smiling I appreciate the smile, and there's the guy who was chasing me earlier, and then someone impossibly hot walks right down the stairs, dark hair with sideburns, red shirt, I motion him into a booth but he looks confused, then I say come in and he follows. This is the best moment really, when everything flows from one guy to the next I mean this is the potential of public sex, it's why I can't possibly give it up, even if my chances are 50 to 1 to get there I'll still keep trying. This guy wants to know what I'm on, I'm familiar with his discomfort. Until I grab his head and it's all about making out in the booth and then later I've even got him pressed against the wall in the hallway, liquor breath maybe he wants some of what I've got I've got something yes I've got something I've got it now I've got it yes please don't take it away.

Later, much later, I'm on craigslist salivating over cocks in underwear without text, cocks out of underwear looking for mouths, hopefully mine, but I'm only sending photos of myself with personality: the one of me with curls sculpted in place and I'm biting into a piece of toast. Of course I should've just headed over to the Nob Hill Theatre video booths, it's Saturday night and at least there'd be someone there, or I could walk in circles through that hallway but now it's 2:08 a.m., the video booths close at 2:30 so maybe I'd get there with five minutes to use the bathroom, blow my nose, walk around in an almost-circle then back up the stairs and out the door. Then walking home through all the drunk tourists and desperate addicts waiting for change. In the background, there's some sort of traffic signal out of whack, chirping in threes.

On the free phone sex line, this guy says where are you? I say downtown. He says downtown—you think the whole world is San Francisco, don't you? I say no, I don't think the whole world is San Francisco. He says you think the whole world is San Francisco—you came here to be gay, didn't you? I say I didn't come here to be gay.

I don't say: I came here to be queer.

He says why couldn't you stay in the town where you came from and stick it out? He's screaming at me like he's daring me to be a man, why couldn't I be a man and stick it out.

I change my tone of voice: bitch you want my load, ooh girl my sweet sweet honey load? He hangs up. I'm actually really worked up, why am I so worked up?

I call the line again, and there he is. Hi sweetheart, he says. Sweetheart?

This time he wants to fuck me, he wants to do it the way it's supposed to be done—first he gets me all warmed up, then fingers, then I'm begging him. But you sound like you're on meth, he says—are you on meth, you're on meth aren't you you're on meth I can tell you're on meth aren't you. I say I'm not on anything—I don't even drink. He says you're drinking, you sound a little loopy, I can tell you're drinking. I say I am a little loopy, but I'm not drinking. Our time on the free line runs out and I'm spared this guy's ranting, then a few guys who like to hang up really quick when the tiniest thing is wrong like how you say hello and then this guy is back again, he says I like your voice, I can tell you're really sweet—you are really sweet, aren't you?

I'm waiting for the bus, and some guy stares right at me, but when I look for his eyes again he's already past—I'm looking at his back. No one turns around anymore, that's what you do online, hurting your neck again. I'm wondering about the difference between cruising someone's look and cruising. I always assume they're clocking the fashion, studying the hair, taking it all in, making notes for the folks back home. But what about when the eyes open wide with excitement—is that an appreciation of color and contrast, texture and pattern, or the possibility of our lips interlocked? I don't know if I'll ever figure it out.

But now I'm back at the Nob Hill Theatre. The guy at the front counter says hello like I was just there yesterday, the problem is that even though it's been a month it still feels that way. Walking around in circles thinking I should leave now I really should leave now I've been here too long I should leave now. You want to know about the porn: Dutch boys barebacking—that one's okay until they start to look too skinny and anxious, piled one next to the other in fucking pairs, a brothel importing fresh Eastern Europeans. Then there's big-budget LA porn, puffed-up guys with insanely big dicks: is that really—and no, really? My favorite is two guys cruising on an airplane, one guy's jerking off and the other guy's looking anxiously over his shoulder at the imagined passengers, his girlfriend asleep between them but then I accidentally switch to some guy wrapped in latex, whimpering, and when I'm back the two guys on the plane are naked in another row of seats and where are the other passengers? It's not exciting anymore.

I leave, and outside this guy does a double-take, turns around and says well you're certainly a faggot, a faggot with a circus for pants you're a faggot if I've ever seen a faggot. He's so close that I'm laughing. All of his gestures are reading straight, but he says: Where are you going? I say I don't know. He says I'm going somewhere to do drugs. His eyes bugging in and out and he's swaying, the tweaker across the street is yelling I took care of you! This guy says no, I took care of you!

He touches the front of my pants—why are you in such a good mood, you're a mess your fly's open, are you a stripper here? I'm laughing, zipping my fly. I say it won't last that long, I'll get home and I'll be depressed. I grab him playfully and kiss the back of his neck, he sort of turns around and then I kiss his neck from the front too. He says what are you on?

I'm laughing and he says oh—everything, what do you mean what am I on—everything! The tweaker is yelling from the distance, this guy yells GO AWAY. I say who's that tweaker? He says I'm gonna hit you in the head, and he holds two plastic bottles in the air, I step back. I say what's that? He says silicon—I say what are you going to do with silicon? He says I work at Lucas Films, I'm gonna hit you in the head—go away.

I start walking downhill and maybe he has friends who show up and they're laughing and pointing in my direction. I'm wondering if he thought I was crazy because I was flirting with him after he kept calling me faggot. I guess that was kind of weird, but cruising spaces are barely different than some homophobe on the street, demanding your adherence to the worst norms of masculinity unless you want your head bashed in I mean a blowjob. I'm walking slowly to appreciate the few minutes I have before collapse, taking pictures of the way light reflects through the glittery letters on the Victoria's Secret window, just the colors up close like distorted chandeliers. Then I'm at the bus stop looking at those terrible digital displays they've installed that tell you how long you have to wait but it's always longer—this one says: NEXT BUS IN 72 MINUTES.

The next day there's my body and the way the sun makes me squint into exhaustion until even the fresh air is too much. I'm somewhere between everything and nothing, and it's something about the way the air hits me so cool and moist I'm flooded with memories of when I first came to San Francisco, that time on Haight Street when I was sitting on the sidewalk writing in my journal and Sam walked up, he thought I was a Haight Street kid and sure, there I was sitting on the sidewalk in all my dyed-hair glory, telling him how crystal made me so sad I didn't want to do crystal. He invited me home, I can't remember if this was the first time we'd had sex or if it had already happened—he said I don't have to fuck you it's not something I have to do. I wanted to get it over with I would never have told him it was the first time. I was embarrassed— I was already nineteen. The room got so hot it was like I was burning up, his dick slipped out he said oh there's blood on the condom. I said it's been a while and then he showed me different literary magazines, I liked the way his face got all red.

Sometimes I walk on the streets so gorgeous with decaying old buildings and other people's memories, I stare into any eyes that come my way to see if they are those eyes but it so rarely happens that way anymore. Everything has been emptied out. It's common to lament the loss of 1970s gay sexual culture, but I have no nostalgia for something I never experienced. I actually miss the possibilities of the 1990s, when I did experience the hope of transcendence through an engagement with gestures of public desire. Of course it was never enough, the connections far sparser than they should have been, even in the crowded spaces clambering for that embrace of cock down throat or hand on neck or tongue to tongue, dark sky up above or the back walls of some bar like a shelter: when I cruised, and it was actually fun.

But now I'm on craigslist—I figure why not post what I'm looking for, I mean post that I don't know what I'm looking for: "Maybe a childlike vulnerability in my eyes there's a gentleness." I add pictures of a glowing fluorescent tube on a black ceiling, red lights on another ceiling, blurred colors, the back of my head with my orange paisley sweater. One person responds, I'm not sure if I'm attracted to him but I say so anyway. He doesn't reply. Then I'm looking at the postings again, again and again and again until I realize I need to ban myself until next year—maybe I should try two years, but I like to pick goals that I'll succeed at. I've already banned myself from Blow Buddies until January, that was back in June and I thought maybe I'd get to January and never want to go again. I thought maybe I'd have figured out something else. I guess I still have a month and a half, but right now I'm thinking I'll be there as soon as the new year comes around. At least if I go back, then I'll know whether I have to ban myself again.

Waking up from a dream where my father's showing me how arousal works, his dick grinding into his pants he's thrusting like he's fucking someone in his jeans it's like a movie where he's standing in the sun the whole time, everything a '70s porn model could want, the light shining down I reach for his hand to place it against my dick and that's when I come, just like that in my own jeans like his. Waking up, I'm thinking when was the last time I wore jeans? Blue jeans, only for tricks or briefly when I was thirteen, I acid-washed them with Clorox but they never looked right. Really I'm thinking at least he's dead so that can't happen, but then I realize I actually did come, not just in the dream, this stickiness between my legs that makes me desperate and angry—desperate because why can't I just have good sex, angry because here he is again he'll always be here.

So I'm at the Nob Hill Theatre, wondering if there's anything I can gain from this experience of standing against the wall that's most comfortable, now that I'm sick of walking in circles. Maybe I'll feel better if I walk around and sing along to the music: "You're as COLD as ice, you're as cold as ice, you're as cold as ice, I know—oh." Right into the eyes of the guy with curly hair who won't look at me after that.

But the real story is the boy who's working the register at the health food store, I'm looking at him and he's looking at me and even if he doesn't look straight there are all sorts of art school straight boys working at health food stores and sometimes even cruising me until I get up close and they say: Hey man. But this boy's definitely watching me while he's ringing up someone's groceries, distracted by focusing on what I'm saying—what am I saying? Something about the music and don't they get to choose it because the woman ringing me up is complaining why not Motown, a customer is requesting Motown he's from Detroit. Meanwhile, my gaze shifts to the other register, I should've gone over there but it was too crowded. Instead I wave like I'm even farther away and say hi! Hi, he says. I say you're really hot—do you want to go on a date? All that matters is that I say exactly what I'm thinking and then I feel that rush like I'm a little kid and I can just be me and it's okay.

I'm trying to get to the place where my sexuality doesn't feel so separate from the visions that inspire me, where it's not just moments so charged like a sudden burst of everything I need. Like I'm filled with possibility it's me I'm everywhere at once. Except there are rules and I know them—don't talk don't smile don't laugh. Sex with guys who can't deal with any exchange past the physical, sometimes not even the physical. If we talk afterwards, and I say my name's Mattilda, often these guys demand: What's your real name? As if they've never heard of self-determination.

Sometimes I wish I could let go of sex, maybe desire would become something else like lying in the grass and holding the sky. But then I'm at Steamworks, wondering what it would mean if we all started crying at the same time. This super-skinny guy comes up to me and says I find you extremely attractive, it would please me if I could kiss you—overly formal and awkward I'm guessing English isn't his first language. I kiss him on the lips and he asks me if I want to go to his room— no, I say—I'm tired, I think I'm going to leave. Then he comes back around, this nervousness that feels submissive even in its assertiveness, he says do you want to go into my room and rest? I can tell that rest means he'll be touching me super-softly like I'm a bird, which is what he's doing now and it makes me tense but I say that's sweet, but no thanks.

Maybe there is a sweetness to him, at least in the way that he doesn't seem shady although part of that might just be inexperience—he looks awfully young, what will he be like in twenty years? And I can't help thinking about how maybe he's performing Asianness and whether that's for the benefit of my perceived whiteness, how this relates to a masculinity I suddenly embody in these spaces and whether all of this forms the reasons I'm not attracted to him. Or whether it's just the way he touches me.

After I eat something, I'm walking around again until I notice the guy with the shaved head—there's something about the way he's breathing that means he's breathing for me I mean differently for me and I realize he was cruising me really hard earlier but from the distance and I wasn't sure I was feeling anything. Now I'm feeling like I need to get on my knees but I don't want to be rude and pull his dick away from the guy down below who's mostly looking at me, I can't tell if it's because he wants my dick or because he wants to know if I want to suck this guy's dick so I try to let him know with my eyes.

The guy from earlier is watching from a distance that's maybe supposed to be discreet but it just looks weird, I motion him over while I'm hugging this other guy and then he kisses me on the cheek too softly almost like a child it makes me feel awkward I kiss him on the neck anyway then he's touching me with only the very outer surfaces of his fingertips and I move my head to the other side so he can't reach. I'm struck by the way language isn't used in this space and the way I'm imprisoned by that and complicit too, but then he's gone and I feel shady except then the other guy's dick is available so that's all I'm thinking about, way past the point when I should stand up because I'm hurting my neck I mean not now but my neck will hurt later right now it's just yes, this is what desire feels like I still don't understand but this is it I know.

I've been trying to think of a particular phrase, something like it's over but grander and more eloquent like the love is gone but I never thought it was love. So I just get stuck trying to figure out how to say that I don't know if there's any hope for me in public sex anymore. I do think things have changed, especially the way guys walk around with a shopping list like they're checking off boxes and that's the influence of the internet but also maybe I've changed. Maybe I need something else.

I understand why so many fags give up on sex, or give up hoping that sex will become anything other than something lost, over and over again this loss or maybe I mean lack, this sense that something is lacking and some people go to great lengths to keep it that way. Others just follow the rules, and the rest of us slowly lose our sense that sex will ever illuminate anything.

When I was a hooker I became so accustomed to performing a certain kind of masculinity, an uncomplicated emotional facade, a clean-cut normalcy, detachment even in the midst of physical passion: How do I get him off? What time is it? Will we be done soon? This also served me in the general world of gay sexual culture. In some ways it used to make me feel hopeful that I could find beauty with people who might shun me in another realm. In some ways it helped that we had little in common except these lips, this tongue, these hands, those eyes, oh this embrace those legs that cock his sweat the texture of his ears his teeth the roof of his mouth that stubble these arms yes these arms: there's something about the things you can see with that sudden intimacy, the shift of breath and perspective. I never accepted the limitations, and I was always aware they existed in dramatic and desperate ways, but still that embrace maybe it was worth it.

Even with those tricks where I'd start and think oh no, how am I going to do it? And then when I would really go there, deep into the physical connection I mean it could become something we would savor and share and then it was over. He might go back to his job figuring out how to deport undocumented immigrants or how to help multinational corporations plunder indigenous resources, so yes there could be something grotesque about my job serving his needs, but still the way my mind could shift into my body a sudden calm a lightness an opening. What's shifted now is that I'm not sure any of it is worth the sadness, the distance, the desperation, the yearning for something else, the lack of potential. Now, in the sexual spaces where so much shutting off is required, I find myself exhausted just being there. So exhausted that I can hardly function. And then I can't figure out what's desire and what's loneliness, what's performance and what's play. I can't even figure out what I want.

It's January and yes, I'm back at Blow Buddies. They're playing "Here Comes the Rain Again," but it's not the Eurythmics it's a cover of the song with a male vocalist that's even more overwrought than the original, like you can hear the ocean in the circuit beats and I'm hugging this guy and it's funny because this is when the kissing gets really good, but it's still not as good as the music wants it to be. I'm holding on to find what's next I'm not quite there until he starts scratching my back and that's what really makes me smile and giggle like I'm humming then he's kissing my neck my eye resting inside his ear just when "I want to dive into your ocean" comes on again and it's funny like looking into a conch shell except my eyes are closed so I can feel things better.

ANYONE YOU COME INTO
CONTACT WITH

I met Johanna at a party in New York in 1998—actually I was talking to her boyfriend first, barrettes in his dyed black hair and painted nails, I was trying to figure out if he was a fag or if he was from Olympia. Johanna came over, and he introduced her. To his credit, he didn't say: This is my girlfriend. Or: This is my partner. Just: This is Johanna.

Johanna was tall and blonde, and she spoke with a high breathy voice that confused me at first because I didn't know any women who talked that way, but after a moment or two our conversation felt conspiratorial in the way that meant we were going to become friends. When she came to my first reading in New York, she brought a friend in a leopard print coat named Kathy, and after the reading we went to dinner but Kathy had to go home. We hugged goodbye and Andy was standing there like someone had just smacked him in the face. Afterwards, he said Mattilda, I'm seeing stars!

What do you mean, I said. Andy said Mattilda, Kathleen Hanna came to your reading. That wasn't Kathleen Hanna, I said—her name was Kathy. Andy said Mattilda, that was Kathleen Hanna, and I figured he must be right because Kathleen Hanna changed his life, changed a lot of people's lives actually, but by the time I found out about her music and all the other Riot Grrrl bands, that wasn't the kind of music I liked anymore. Punk was something I was trying to be in high school, I went to Fugazi shows and swayed in the back corner, as far away from the slamming as possible. I had pretty much every album by The Clash, and even wrote a story named after their song "Stay Free" that described the kind of friendships I fantasized about, "We met / when we were at school / never took no shit from no one." But I was too much of a faggot to be accepted as punk, this was DC at the end of the '80s and I wasn't out I mean I didn't know anyone who was but everyone knew about me.

When I discovered dance music, it was such a relief—I didn't have to feel like an alien just because I wanted to look styley and twirl around instead of slamming into people. But then when I got to San Francisco in 1992, I was suddenly surrounded by music that called itself punk again, punk music and slam-dancing, except now it was queers who were slamming, queers who sneered at any mention of house, techno—so repetitive, they would say, but really they were saying only fags listen to that, the wrong kind of fags. So I danced to house but lived in a different world, a world of dykes and a few fags who held each other and talked about rape and feminism and thrift stores and veganism and surviving childhood abuse. We made zines and chapbooks and dyed our hair and painted our nails and wrote manifestos and stuck nails through our ears and organized protests and competed with one another for shoplifting excess, shared recipes and tips on sexual health and got angry and crazy and depressed together, but we were in San Francisco so we looked down on Riot Grrrl and everything else we associated with Olympia, and even Kathleen Hanna—we thought we were tougher and smarter and more original. By this point I lived for house music, so of course that's when people decided I was punk. Maybe it was because I made out with boys at a dyke bar where we danced to Chumbawamba and Hole and X-Ray Spex and God Is My Co-Pilot and Bratmobile, or because I dyed my hair crazy colors and wore lots of dangly silver earrings and the rest of the things I was afraid to wear in high school, like plaid pants and combat boots. Or maybe because I didn't care anymore—the rules are different when you finally get away.

Or maybe it was because activism mattered so much to me: ACT UP meetings had become the most important thing in my life. ACT UP meant politicizing everything, and that's what queer meant to me. You learned by absorbing the room—generations of activism and relationships and contrasting ways of communicating, the laughter between tense moments, the process of committees and affinity groups and consensus. ACT UP meant fighting AIDS because everyone was dying, and it also meant making connections—between government neglect of people with AIDS and structural homophobia and racism; between the US war machine and the lack of funding for health care; between misogyny and the absence of resources for women with AIDS; between the war on drugs and the abandonment of HIV-positive drug addicts and prisoners. There were several other direct action groups in San Francisco at the time, and ACT UP ended up doing a lot of coalition actions with BACORR, the Bay Area Coalition for Our Reproductive Rights; and RAW, Roots Against War, which was people of color against US imperialism; and then WAC, the Women's

Action Coalition. These coalitions basically meant that six of us got together, mostly the youngest people in each group. We were the ones with the energy to take on extra work—we were ready to make flyers and go out wheatpasting and carrying torches through the streets.

I don't remember anyone in ACT UP ever saying oh, you're so young, and that meant a lot to me too. I was already going to bars and saying I was twenty-three when I was in high school, and then when I moved to San Francisco this guy who was twenty-six took me out to the Café San Marcos, which was the only dyke bar in the Castro, but they had a dance floor so fags went there too, and then we were standing on the balcony and he asked me how old I was, I said nineteen and he started freaking out, pulling people over and saying can you believe it, can you believe he's nineteen? So after that I was twenty-three again, at least in bars.

The gay clubs were always about 95% fags and only a few dykes, or if they were mixed that meant straight with a few dyke or fag club kids, but even if there were only six or seven dykes that was who I became friends with. Even at the places where everything was about attitude, which was most places except when it got late and then it was just about dancing to the sky with crystal in the air. But there was also Junk, which was the only club where it felt like everything at once—dancing, and politics, and sex.

At Junk I didn't want drugs, I didn't even drink because somehow it felt like there in that bar we were creating a life together. A bunch of us would head over right after ACT UP and it was the reverse of the other clubs so mostly dykes and a few fags scattered around, although this was the only bar where I actually picked up guys on a regular basis. There was even a point where I decided I would go home with someone every week, and it actually worked, for a little while at least. And I met Derek there, Derek who was always eating whole cloves of raw garlic and he made me think of the person I was trying to become and we made out on the dance floor, all that garlic and sweat. I went back to his apartment behind the sausage factory that night, they had to keep the windows closed during the day because otherwise the sausage smell would overwhelm everything. Pretty soon I was going there all the time and people on the street which was really an alley would throw glass bottles at me, or not really at me but in my direction, they never hit me but shattered in front of me or behind me and I pretended not to notice. Maybe one of them did hit me once: I kept walking.

But actually that time I went home with Derek after Junk wasn't the first time we met—there was a café down the street, where we'd stare at each other but not say anything. I thought he was hot but snotty so mostly I'd stare at the duct tape on the back of his leather jacket, which reminded me of one of the first guys I had a crush on: I'd spent a lot of time staring at the back of his leather jacket.

Eventually Derek and I would say hi and smile and we knew each other's names, but it was at Junk where we were sweating so close until we were sweating together. I remember waking up in his bed and then going into the kitchen where Derek was always doing something really involved like making sourdough bread from a starter he'd concocted himself from all kinds of rotten who-knows-what but half the time we were making out in the way that your whole head becomes your tongue and your nose and the other person's hands it was so much fun to hold hands on the street and hold each other in bed we were holding everything.

Sometimes Derek would twist his head around like he was trying to snap it off or he'd eat a whole pint of Rice Dream and then vomit it back into the container and eat it again. He would keep jars of piss under the bed so he didn't have to get up in the middle of the night and then sometimes his whole room would start to smell like piss but this was what love meant to me, seeing these things and loving them and I almost forgot to talk about the laughing, sometimes Derek would get out of control with laughing his whole face all red and then I would start laughing and then he would say stop, it hurts, but then we couldn't stop it was hard to breathe but still we were laughing, no stop, stop! We would talk for hours and hours, days really, we'd go to bed and then wake up and just keep talking which was dreaming and learning and breathing and yearning all at once. Derek's father had kicked him out of the house when he was fifteen because he had a mohawk and that was ten years before we met so he had more stories to tell, at least more stories about the past because mine were still mostly about the future, although in those days everything could change in two months.

Like when I went to the March on Washington in 1993 to do civil disobedience with ACT UP for universal health care and we expected hundreds of people but we only ended up with a few dozen. At an earlier ACT UP demo I'd met this boy from Michigan, and we ended up going to protests together, ran through the DC streets at night dancing to RuPaul's "Supermodel" even though we knew it was cheesy, and then making out with anyone we thought was hot. DC, where suddenly there were a million white gay people in white t-shirts applying for Community Spirit credit cards. Gays in the military was the big issue and what could be more horrifying but here's the thing: the freaks actually found one another—we were so alienated that we went right up and said hi, I like your hair, I mean that's what people said to me at least, since my hair was purple and red and green. And I met Zee, the boy from

Michigan with a shaved head and the cutest little nose ring like a tiny dot that kind of matched the braces he tried to hide since who had braces at nineteen but I thought they were cute and he ended up becoming my first boyfriend, since Derek and I never called ourselves that. I also met JoAnne who later became my closest friend, and even Chrissie Contagious, who was on ecstasy screaming naked from a tree in Dupont Circle.

And then after all the festivities ended there were a few fags with suitcases, and more trash in the streets, and I was making out with Zee in Georgetown, right in front of the all-night restaurant where I used to go after clubs and warehouse parties in high school. Zee and I even went to The Vault, one of the clubs from my high school days and I still liked the music, actually it was better, and afterwards we were making out in Georgetown—that never happened in high school I mean I couldn't even imagine. Two guys who looked like Georgetown University students came up and said what are you doing? Kissing, I said, and went back to it, and remember how I said everything could change in two months? But sometimes it changed in two days. Or two minutes.

They sprayed something in my eyes and then I was screaming it hurt so much I wasn't sure I could see and Zee and I went into the 24-hour restaurant—in the bathroom I was throwing water on my face it was so red it looked like spray paint. And they said take this outside, the people working at the restaurant. You need to take this outside. So then we were trying to hail a cab but no cab would stop, I guess I must have looked that bad and when we finally got to the hospital they made me lie down on the table and they put tubes in my eyes and pumped in saline for 45 minutes to flush out the pepper spray, that's what they said it was: they said it was a good thing I came right to the hospital because otherwise I might've lost my vision.

The next day my parents asked: Why do you have to be so overt?

Back in San Francisco, I did go to a Bikini Kill show once—we arrived early because the space was small and we were worried it would get too crowded—everyone was waiting for Kathleen Hanna to get in a fight with some macho guy, they kept yelling KICK HIS ASS. I hated fights it was depressing. Oh, and also people were whispering: Is she, or isn't she? As in queer. But I thought I was going to write about New York.

So I met Johanna at a party in 1998, but what was I doing at a party? I never really liked parties, even in high school they were boring, but this was Dasha's party—I must've met her at Dumba, the anarchist space in Brooklyn started by four people who wanted to create an alternative to the misogyny and homophobia at ABC No Rio, the storied anarchist space on the Lower East Side where punk bands often played. I met Gina at Dumba too, I thought she was so cute with her shaved head and lip ring and we would flirt with each other in the way that dykes and fags flirt. Later she lived at Dumba or maybe we met when she was already living there, but anyway Dumba kind of became a space for a queer outsider culture that didn't really exist elsewhere in New York.

That's when I was looking for activists again—I'd taken a break from direct action for several years, I was trying to figure out how to engage in activist groups without taking everyone's anger into my body. That's the pattern I'd noticed in San Francisco after I remembered I was sexually abused, before then I thought it was okay because I knew these people really weren't angry at me, they were angry about the issues.

In ACT UP meetings you had to be ready for someone to tear you to shreds any time you said something—no, you didn't have a right to speak about people with AIDS if you weren't HIV-positive, or to talk about women with HIV if you weren't a woman, and I'm not sure who had the right to talk about prisoners with AIDS, because none of us were in prison, and definitely if you said something kind of wishy-washy or unprocessed then several people would jump on you at once. You had to become incredibly meticulous, critical, and alert in order to say anything—luckily I was good at that. And it was an emergency, we were trying to save people's lives.

But then I was part of a new activist group where we held a sleep-out on the steps of the mayor's house to call attention to the Matrix Program, his corporate-backed plan to rid downtown San Francisco of homeless people, we arrived with sleeping bags and got arrested pretty quickly but we got a lot of press. Activists from RAW had invited specific people from other groups to join them in challenging Matrix, and after our sleepover we started holding meetings at the Coalition on Homelessness to figure out what to do next. We were going to target Gap because Don Fisher, the head of Gap, was one of the big funders behind Matrix, but first we had to agree on our decision-making process, if it was going to be democratic majority or consensus.

I was the person most in favor of consensus, since I thought it worked so smoothly in ACT UP—but most people didn't have that experience: they thought consensus was an unworkable fantasy. There were others who were in favor of consensus, but they didn't say anything during meetings because of the way the people with the most power would get up and literally start screaming at me: How could you even think of consensus we'll never get anything done you're holding up the group there are important things we have to accomplish.

Since we hadn't decided on our process, we kind of had to use consensus at first anyway. I would sit there so calmly and describe how consensus worked in ACT UP, how it was the best way to ensure that everyone could participate in decision-making. And then people would stand up and attack me. And after a few of these meetings I realized oh, actually it's not okay when people tear each other to shreds, I mean it's not okay for me because I hold it all in my body. Just like with my father's rage.

This was the period where sometimes I thought my father was following me down the street, at night I worried he was under the bed, behind the curtains with an axe, I would ask my roommate Camelia to look. She was the first incest survivor I'd met, and it was her mother who was a dyke who had abused her and this took apart a lot of illusions at once.

Camelia would look under my bed and say no, there's no one there. Sometimes I would wake up in the middle of the night and everything in my room was my father's eyes I needed to get up to turn on the light but I was too scared, all I could do was lie there in terror. Or I would be sitting on the bus and suddenly I couldn't figure out what people were doing, how they were going on with their lives and then I would remember oh, we're on the bus, I can get off the bus and then when I got off I would tell myself no, my father is not following me, my father is not following me down the street, my father isn't even in San Francisco. But then I would get that sudden panic anyway, just before turning around and I would shake and stop breathing at the same time, my whole body covered in sweat but okay, okay, it's not my father, there's no one there.

When I moved to New York in 1997, it was harder to find people—you needed to know someone in order to know someone. I knew Ananda through Andy, and she invited me to join a group called the Fuck the Mayor Collective although the name kept changing. It was a small group of queers who made stickers exposing Giuliani's quality-of-life campaign as a brutal push to gentrify neighborhoods in Manhattan previously considered unsafe for tourism and real estate profiteering, while dismantling social services, criminalizing people of color, and removing any hint of sexual culture from the public realm. I got involved right before the group began planning a big event called Gay Shame—the idea was to create a radical alternative for queers to make our own culture and share strategies for resistance instead of swallowing the corporate pride agenda. I volunteered to MC the event, which really did open up space for queer troublemaking. Most people there were young and white, but still we were dedicated to a queer analysis that foregrounded race and class, and Dumba became a place where we could find something, or someone, or sometimes nothing but punk bands, and you already know how I felt about punk bands, but at least they weren't the same nothing that surrounded us on the billboards inside people's hearts.

I guess I met people at Dumba—that's helpful—I'm trying to figure out where to meet people now. Anyway, the good thing about meeting Johanna was that we were both driven but not driven like most of New York—Prada shoes and a penthouse—I was driven to figure out how to use radical queer direct action to confront the violence of the Giuliani regime, and public sex as a way to escape and connect and writing as a way to connect and escape, and Johanna was a painter and zine-maker and then she started making music with Kathleen. We both did drugs, but didn't really want to do drugs, except when we were doing them, or maybe Johanna did, but I didn't. We didn't really go out together, because Johanna mostly went to straight hipster parties and I mostly went to sceney East Village gay bars, so instead when we got together we talked a lot, about sex work and sex outside of work and what was the difference, and we talked about New York and all of its layers of violence and then the West Coast since that was where Johanna was from and I felt like I was from the West Coast too, even though I grew up in DC I really grew up in San Francisco.

I never believed that whole West Coast–East Coast thing until I moved to New York where there was no flamboyance except money. Whatever the trend of the moment, everyone in New York was working it. If you met someone at a bar, the first question they would ask was: What do you do? Or, they would decide ahead of time, and say: Are you a stylist? Or: Are you in fashion? I mean that's what they would say to me.

But after Gay Shame, June of 1998, I was finally finding activists in New York, and then, in October, when the murder of Matthew Shepard became front-page news, a few people decided that something angry had to happen immediately. They called everyone they knew, and in just a few days about twenty of us planned a political funeral where we would march through the streets in midtown at rush hour in order to interrupt business as usual and broadcast our rage. We were invoking a history of political funerals in ACT UP: it was important to distinguish this protest from a vigil, where everyone is silent. We were not interested in being silent.

We went out and flyered every gay bar we could get to, as if this was the '70s and bars were still community spaces—we expected 1,000 people if we were really successful, but we actually ended up with 10,000. That was because of the internet too, but we didn't really know that yet. Or I didn't. The cops started attacking us instead of letting us march in the street so most of the marshals got arrested right away, and I was the one person in charge of front-to-back communication, this was before all my physical pain started. Or before I noticed.

I was running back and forth through the crowd as the cops were swinging their clubs and charging us on horseback and in the end I remember standing in Madison Square Park, hours later when there were maybe only two other marshals left. We held a press conference, and I stood next to a protester with blood dripping down his face, blood from police batons and we were on all the TV stations saying: This is what happens when queers try to protest homophobic violence.

Afterwards, we tried to create a large-scale radical queer activist group, but we got stuck in endless discussions about what our mission statement and tactics would be and the meetings became smaller and smaller. Some of us formed an affinity group called Fed Up Queers to do targeted actions— at first the idea was that we would only meet when someone came up with an idea for an action, so we wouldn't get bogged down in process. But then we went from one action to the next, since someone always had an idea, sometimes there were several ideas at once and we were always meeting.

When Amadou Diallo, an unarmed West African man, was gunned down in a hail of forty-one NYPD bullets, there were protests but no one was getting arrested and we decided to raise the stakes. We wanted to block the Brooklyn Bridge during rush hour, but we only had eight people who could risk arrest so we said okay, we'll block the bridge with eight people. We measured the width of the bridge, bought chain so that we could cover several hundred feet, scouted the location, planned it all out. But when we got there, we found cops waiting in the exact spot we'd chosen. Since this was a covert action, we had obviously been infiltrated but we didn't think about that right away, instead we went to plan B but plan B wasn't possible either. So we chained ourselves across Broadway in rush-hour traffic, except the person forming the middle link somehow disappeared—that was the infiltrator, the only time in an activist group when we've know for sure.

We blocked the street anyway; the chains made it more dramatic because the cops had to bring out electric saws to get the locks off, and we were right near the permitted demonstration organized by black church leaders, the action we were supporting. So we were lying in the freezing cold February streets with reporters bending over to ask what a bunch of queers, most of us white, could possibly be doing blocking traffic. That's not what they said exactly, but it's what they meant. I said we're here because unarmed people of color are being gunned down on the streets of New York, and it's a state of emergency.

It was a state of emergency. With direct action, it's always a state of emergency and that's good because you're on alert, ready to intervene. And it's hard because you can never do enough. It's why I got involved in Queeruption, which started with four people in a car on the way back from a queer writer's conference: Scott, Kathryn, Jesse and me. And Taylor in Boston. All of the others had attended anarchist gatherings where they felt inspired by the politics but marginalized as queers, and they wanted to organize a queer anarchist convergence. I wasn't that interested because it didn't sound like direct action, and I wasn't even sure I was an anarchist—I'd never felt comfortable in anarchist spaces because they'd always felt so straight and male. But I guess that was the point.

We started holding weekly meetings at Bluestockings, the feminist bookstore Kathryn had founded. We decided Queeruption would take place over Columbus Day weekend in 1999, so I figured we needed an anti-imperialist direct action: I suggested we target the Statue of Liberty as a symbol of US colonialism, connecting NYPD murders of unarmed people of color, the US occupation of the Puerto Rican island of Vieques, police attacks on queers at protests in New York, and the never-ending crackdown on public sex—we planned to bring hundreds of queers to New York, so what could be a better opportunity to make these connections?

We actually started to plan this out, the few people who were interested—this was before activists were regularly branded as terrorists: we even wondered if we could get Lady Liberty to drip blood-red paint; would we occupy the statue, or should we try for an elaborate banner drop? We figured out theatrical stunts for people who didn't want to get arrested, talked about whether we should do something on the ferry or wait until we got to the island. Then I had to leave for a trip to the West Coast, so I told the direct action working group to go ahead and plan the action without me.

When I got back, no one had planned anything because the larger group had decided our action wasn't queer enough. But then I was at a Fed Up Queers meeting, or I guess it wasn't officially a Fed Up Queers meeting because our meetings weren't open to the public, but it was something related, and some guy showed up in office clothes like some of the gay men who came to the Matthew Shepard political funeral, the gay men who I thought might become politicized after suffering police violence but mostly that didn't happen. Anyway, this guy told us about one night when he was cruising the Ramble in Central Park, and he went behind a bush to piss, and behind the bush there was a cop who arrested him for public indecency. In jail, the guards incited the other prisoners against him and they raped him while holding a razor blade at his neck; soon after he got out of jail he tested HIV-positive.

This guy was asking us for help—he didn't know us, or even know much about our politics and in a way that made it more important. I realized oh, this could be the Queeruption action—it was obviously queer, right? And so, at the next general meeting I proposed the idea: we would take back the park with a queer carnival to connect the entrapment of gay men while cruising with the arrests of trans women on prostitution charges just for hanging out on the street, with police targeting of queer activists at protests—all of these were attacks on queer visibility. We would challenge the cops in the park and at the same time create our own idealized queer space for the evening, a place where queers of all genders could cruise together and celebrate with the pageantry and play of public confrontation.

But then Kathryn said: I don't understand how this action relates to lesbians. And since most of the people in the room were lesbians who were there because of Kathryn, the proposal went down. You see how activism works. This was so different from organizing with Fed Up Queers—that group was mostly dykes too, but no one ever asked: How does this action relate to me? Because we knew that wasn't the point.

Don't get me wrong—there was plenty of drama in Fed Up Queers, but a different kind of drama. People would get in screaming fights about what time we should meet or the wording of a flyer, but then afterwards you would realize they were really arguing because somebody was sleeping with someone's ex-girlfriend. I didn't find this out until much later because I didn't have a history with these people: we were making our own history but that was different.

Kathryn and I did have a history—she was the one who'd invited me to help plan the Matthew Shepard political funeral, and then we were always in conversation while she got ready to open Bluestockings, and she and Scott and I bonded because we were all vegan, there weren't many vegans in New York. Especially not vegan queers. So I sat down with Kathryn and figured out how to get her support, which meant the support of the group, and then I organized pretty much every aspect of the action and basically harassed people into going, and we actually ended up with over a hundred people. The crowd was multi-gendered and intergenerational and even included a few Stonewall veterans, Sylvia Rivera and Bob Kohler, and we marched into the park that night with queers in dragged-out glory chanting campy slogans like "Push, push, in the bush!" and we actually found a cop hiding in the bushes. We caught him in the glare of our flashlights and then the head of the park precinct came out to talk to us. I remember yelling: Is that blood on your hands? And we marched back out of the park, no arrests, it was amazing.

But the thing about the months of planning that led up to that action, and the whole Queeruption gathering, was that it drained me so much that afterwards all I could think about was coke, I mean I thought about coke the whole time but I kept thinking not now. Afterwards it was time, time for cocktails and coke. It started at Starlight women's night, partying with the style-dykes and this time some of them actually knew me outside of this other part of me. But then I would end up at the after-hours coke den right around the corner from The Cock, by this point I knew the dealer at The Cock but sometimes he wasn't around and even if he was around sometimes I needed somewhere to go after the bars closed, so I would end up at the coke den talking to these horrible people—straight Eurotrash and decaying lifetime cokeheads and maybe a few gay boys trying not to act too gay because everyone knew the owner was homophobic.

If the owner was there he was usually the only black person, presiding over the bar in over-the-top 1970s pimp style, issuing demands with the wave of one hand while using the other to hold at least one tiny blonde woman close by his side. The blonde woman would snort rails out of his private stash and giggle uncomfortably, and it was hard to tell how much he believed in his performance but you could tell everyone working for him did: they would glance nervously over at him or ask you to put a shirt on because tank tops suddenly weren't allowed or they'd command you to keep buying cocktails so the bar would look legitimate, and that was the most irrational part because the bar was illegal so wouldn't it look more legitimate if they weren't selling alcohol?

I would get so high I couldn't speak it didn't feel high it just felt like someone had locked my brain and these people were talking and then I needed to do another bump. Rush to the bathroom to shit again because of all the laxative in that terrible coke and then back to the bar to act like I could listen. For a few weeks that led to a few months I would even carry coke around, do a bump or two while walking through the East Village and then the lights would become softer and brighter at the same time and once I even did a bump in the bathroom during my queer incest survivors support group.

I can see how the exhaustion had already started, maybe I didn't know about the chronic pain yet, but I definitely knew about the exhaustion. Sometimes I would get so tired in the middle of the day that I would have to sit on the side of the street downtown and close my eyes and try to meditate while everyone streamed by. One time I went over to Johanna's house—she was showing me how to make vegan borscht, which was pretty much the most delicious thing I'd ever tasted, and just before we sat down to eat I went into the bathroom for a quick bump. Did that make the borscht taste better?

Back to Dumba—it turned out Johanna and Kathleen were starting a band with Sadie Benning, and Le Tigre's first show took place there on a freezing, snowy day in the winter of 1999. Or maybe it was 2000. The album says '99, but the crazy thing about that show was that there was a line that went down the street in the snow—there had never been a show like that at Dumba. This huge crowd of riot grrrls, or post-riot grrrls, since Riot Grrrl was over or maybe it wasn't really over because there was this huge crowd. There were people who had driven from Illinois and Ohio just to see Kathleen, and Kathleen kept saying: Who are all these people?

Johanna said Kathleen, there are whole websites dedicated to you, and Kathleen said really? I guess the truth is that every time you do a show, you worry that no one's going to show up, I mean that's what happens for me and maybe that happened for Kathleen too but at the time I just thought she was being fake. I was biased against her because I thought she was a star, the way people lined up afterwards to talk to her but no one else in the band, all these women in leopard print coats with vintage dresses, clunky heels, and big purses.

So what was it about Kathleen Hanna, or Riot Grrrl? Gina says: All that spoken word about getting raped and screaming about it, talking about what you're not supposed to. And: All those songs where Kathleen is shrieking and you're trying to figure out what she's saying and it takes forever but then you eventually figure it out. And: I discovered Riot Grrrl in 1997 so I was a little late but I dropped out of school and went back to my mother's house and bought a drum set and put an ad out to start a band because I needed to hit stuff and scream and get angry and snobby about it. And: Even years later, at that Le Tigre show at Dumba, there was something about staring at Kathleen Hanna putting her guitar strap on, knowing about someone's struggle and seeing them exist anyway and some-times that's how I feel about you.

But I don't know why I'm writing about Riot Grrrl—I mean, Riot Grrrl never meant anything to me. When I lived in Seattle, I never even went to Olympia, although Andy was always trying to get me to go with him. I didn't really understand what was there, except a small town and a bunch of scenesters and I wasn't interested in either. I was never much of a Courtney Love fan, but when I heard that song at the end of the second Hole album where she sings, "When I went to school . . . in Olympi-ah-ah-ah-ah . . . and everyone's the same," I was floored—that's pretty much how I felt about Valencia, the epicenter of dyke hipster San Francisco. So maybe that's why I didn't want to go to Olympia; it sounded like Valencia.

In 1997 before I moved to New York, I traveled from Seattle to San Francisco for a queer writers' conference, where I met Thea Hillman and Elizabeth Stark. We went to a panel where Jennifer Levin said you can't write anything truly great until after you're thirty. Elizabeth, who had just written her first book, raised her hand and said: I'm twenty-six, and I've already written something truly great. I was twenty-three. There were things I knew then that I couldn't possibly know now, and there are things I know now that I couldn't possibly know then.

But back to that first Le Tigre album—I was excited that they were trying to make dance music that was actually political, homemade and messy, and not just empty except for that feeling in your head: they were actually trying to represent something. In one song, they managed to name-drop Leslie Feinberg, Angela Davis, Dorothy Allison, Marlon Riggs, and even Mab Segrest, the author of *Memoirs of a Race Traitor*. David Wojnarowicz. Like in the early '90s, when we would exchange books to start a conversation that was our lives.

After that show at Dumba, Andy said how come you're not in the slideshow? I wasn't sure how I felt about all those names—something was exhilarating but it also felt like cheer-leading. Although I was glad Andy was thinking about me: we all want our place in history. Maybe that's what it felt like Le Tigre was trying to create, even if some of their lyrics were a bit cheesy, like "Giuliani, he's such a fucking jerk." Still they were trying to express this time in our lives, especially on their second album, an EP, where they start by screaming "Get off the internet—I'll meet you in the street," something I can still relate to, and at one point they count off the forty-one bullets the cops used to assassinate Amadou Diallo, making a protest chant into a piece of artistic documentation, and what could be more important? I mean more important for music. I mean they made me think I could make music.

When I moved back to San Francisco at the end of 2000, Le Tigre ended up playing right around the corner from my house—they performed with Chicks on Speed, a band who was becoming part of the art world by satirizing the art world but their beats were wild and broken and that's the kind of sound I craved. I can't remember if this was before or after Le Tigre played at the Michigan Womyn's Music Festival, in spite of the festival's infamous policy of excluding trans women. And right outside stood Camp Trans, organized to protest the exclusion and create an alternative space. But Le Tigre played at the Michigan Womyn's Music Festival. I wonder if they stopped at Camp Trans to say hello, hi, thank you for buying our album.

Even if you don't have idols, there are those moments when your idols let you down. Like that time when I saw Dorothy Allison read, and I rushed to the front to be the first person to talk to her: I wanted to tell her how much she meant to me as a queer incest survivor. She nodded her head but looked right past me to the woman next in line, opened her arms and hugged that woman who she didn't know any more than she knew me, this woman in a line of women, and then there was me and oh how I wanted that hug.

Back to that Le Tigre show in San Francisco, I remember going backstage to say hi—I'd just come from Sugar's birthday party down the street, and when I told her I was going to Le Tigre she said oh, how much are tickets? Twenty dollars. And at that she went off—when she was a teenager in Santa Rosa she wanted to organize a Bikini Kill show, and Bikini Kill had this rule that they would never do a show for more than five dollars. That was an ethic a lot of bands from that time held on to, I remember it from Fugazi shows in DC. And Sugar couldn't find an all-ages space cheap enough in Santa Rosa so she organized the show in a field with a generator, they used car headlights to illuminate the not-quite-stage. Backstage at the Le Tigre show, Zee complimented Kathleen on the slide-show, and Kathleen said oh, we got a new projector, and it was $2,000, but we figured we could just raise ticket prices. It was how she said it—like she didn't even remember that person who insisted on $5 shows. So what about those moments when someone else's idol lets you down?

But Andy says: Mattilda, by the time of that first Le Tigre show at Dumba I had already moved to Berlin.

That's right—you saw them perform in Berlin. But do you remember that zine about class privilege in Riot Grrrl that Mary made, what was her last name?

I can't remember.

That zine called *Rich Girls Make Art*, or maybe it was a manifesto—was it a manifesto or a zine?

That was a drawing in a zine, a drawing of a knife and on the knife it said, "Rich Girls Make Art." I think I have that zine somewhere, along with Kathleen Hanna's zines. I just loved the one where Kathleen defined community as anyone you come into contact with—and I wasn't the type of person who became a fan of anyone, but Kathleen Hanna was an exception.

Speaking of rich girls making art, in 1992 I drove cross-country in my parents' cherry-red Saab 900S, previously the third car in the hierarchy of the driveway, after the newer, fancier Volvo and newer, fancier Saab, safe cars for your kids to drive and that's what I was doing except I'm not sure about the safety part. I was driving out to meet Elyse, the first person who I trusted—we'd met our first year in college where finally I'd realized it was okay to need someone, and we were moving to San Francisco for the summer, just the summer we said but we knew better. We didn't know, but we knew.

We made a list of all the cities that sounded interesting, cut out the ones on the East Coast because they were too close and even Toronto or Chicago didn't sound far enough. We decided against Mexico City because we didn't speak Spanish, and then we just had to choose between Seattle and San Francisco, Elyse always liked flipping coins to make big decisions.

But driving there on my own was a different story, I kept getting so tired that I would see myself falling off the road I mean I wouldn't see myself until I was falling and then I had to swerve back. Coffee and NoDoz and a few stops to stay with the parents of people I didn't know that well, or didn't know at all because it was Elyse who knew their kids but I tried to pretend, and there was this one rest area where I remember stopping, turning up my music to dance which was how I stretched, throwing some trash in the garbage and then working a few dance moves on the sidewalk. This attendant came out of the rest area with rubber gloves going up to his elbows, pulled my trash out of the garbage can and put it in a separate bag, a blue bag like maybe you would use for something bloody in a hospital, and then he looked at me and said: If you don't leave now, I'm going to call the cops. What do you mean, I said—isn't this a rest area? He said: If you don't leave now, I'm going to call the cops.

But then there were the girls at other rest areas who would stop and say: I like your hair! I was working the goth bob except it was magenta, dark tulip the label said, and then in the back the shaved part was fluorescent green, green apple. I ended up getting a flat tire in the middle of Kansas, and I had no idea how to change it; some guy actually stopped his truck and helped me. Then there was a rest area in Wyoming or not quite a rest area but this abandoned store where you could buy gas except there wasn't any gas so I went inside for coffee or Trident. Back then I chewed a lot of Trident, I would eat a whole pack of eighteen pieces in an hour and on my way out these guys behind me said: Should we fuck him first, or just kill him?

Later I remember looking at those crazy plateaus in the desert, mountains that ended too soon and I thought they couldn't possibly be real, someone was hiding something. But I wasn't hiding, that was the good part.

New York had always been my childhood dream but I realized I needed to get much further from DC so I ended up in San Francisco. San Francisco was supposed to be just like New York, except on the West Coast and always foggy, so when I got there I was kind of confused because where were the tall buildings? Elyse had arrived earlier and she'd found us a sublet—we were surprised because people had told us it would be so expensive that we'd have to share a room, but actually we each ended up with our own room for $300, which didn't seem that bad.

I met Elyse at an ice cream social at the school where we both went to escape, except it wasn't what we were trying to escape to and that's how we ended up in San Francisco. Growing up, college was always the answer, the way to get away. I'd gone to the same school from second grade to twelfth, and when you go somewhere like that there are always people who see you exactly like you were in second grade, those ten years don't matter, there's still that kid with his own reading group he was so far ahead, that kid who traded stickers with the girls at recess, that kid with glasses who wanted to be friends with the teachers because other kids were too scary. Sure, by this point you're reading Sartre and obsessing about freedom, going out to clubs with the girls instead of trading stickers, and talking back to all the teachers because you know you've outgrown them. Sure, you're encouraging people, other kids, not to think about parents or teachers or other kids or anyone telling you to die, inside or outside it's the same thing. But the truth is that the first time you really know your effect on people is when you get to college, even though it isn't away in the way you thought it would be, it's still away.

Maybe even at the ice cream social, where you meet Elyse, her big hair chopped short and stuffed into a black-and-white scarf tied around her head like a bandanna, silver hoop earrings. Elyse looks at you with an intensity that makes you think: she's crazy, I like her. You are definitely not eating ice cream, but the social is right by your dorm. You're wearing a Lollapalooza T-shirt, black of course, the first Lollapalooza so people still think it's cool. This is Brown University, where Amy Carter went and you remember in fourth grade when her parents, the president and his wife, sent her to public school in DC, the public school right down the street from your private school; she was in junior high when you were in elementary and people talked about Amy Carter going to Hardy. That's what people talked about in DC, certain parts of DC. Later, at

Brown, Amy Carter got arrested—she got arrested for protesting something.

Soon I would get arrested for protesting, but when I first arrived I felt like people could finally see me. Elyse had grown up in a small town in northern Maine, just across from the Canadian border, a town where people spoke French almost as much as English, a paper mill town; the student population at Brown was larger than the population of her whole hometown. Elyse was raised by a single mother on welfare and now she'd arrived at this school with so much privilege it was hard for her to leave her room. Her room was on frat row, and even though there weren't really frats at Brown there were frats on frat row. I would come over to meet Elyse to go to the dining hall and then the library, where sometimes we'd stay so late we'd get locked in.

Elyse described how her mother, who was a nurse, decided to quit her job because she realized she could work all the time, barely have enough to live on, and rarely see her kids, or go on Aid to Families with Dependent Children and have the time to raise them. I'd grown up in a school where there were senators' kids and no one really cared, a Rothschild and a DuPont and more lawyers and doctors and bureaucrats than you could count. It was the school for guilty liberals, so the people everyone called rich weren't necessarily the people with the most money, but the ones who didn't hide it, who didn't ask if they could borrow a few dollars at recess and then never pay you back. But at Brown there were so many kids who came from boarding school, and that felt like a whole other world. My roommate was the son of a German industrialist, he was twenty-one and had blonde dreads and he didn't like living in the dorms so his parents bought him a house, a huge old mansion so close it was practically on campus, and then a bunch of his European friends moved in with him. So then I had two beds in my dorm room and Elyse stayed over a lot, in the morning I would make her coffee because she had a harder time getting up. At night we'd read our journals to one another and process every detail of our lives—this felt crucial, studying could wait. Until it couldn't wait any longer, and then we'd head over to the smoking room in the basement of the library to gaze at all the other stylish procrastinators.

People must have asked if we were sleeping together, but it didn't matter in the way that it would have mattered before. I wish I could say that our relationship started differently than my relationships with girls in high school, friendships that began when someone had a crush on me and I wanted to make it more, more meant something else. But the truth is that Elyse had a crush on me and we talked about it, talked about sleeping together—we'd always known we were queer, but now we could acknowledge it as a way to dream. Everyone's bisexual was still the way to talk, or everyone's potentially bisexual but soon it became clear that the potential in that direction on my part would probably stay potential.

When you go to a school like Brown, they tell you not to get overwhelmed, not to get overwhelmed because you're used to thinking you're the smartest person but now you're surrounded by so many others who are used to thinking the same thing. I wasn't overwhelmed at all—there were smart people and there were clueless people, just like anywhere else. The difference was that it was actually okay to be smart—smart and creative and strange at the same time, and that made me feel stronger and stranger too.

So let me tell you about SAMA, Students for Aid and Minority Admissions: we took over University Hall, the main administrative building, and it was a big deal. We were protesting the university's policy of openly excluding potential students based on their inability to pay: the university called this need-aware. So we took over the building and 253 people got arrested—the cops brought us downtown to jail in busses, late at night but right to court where they charged us with five misdemeanors, which included a $2,000 fine if convicted. We were there until 2:30 a.m., it must have been a special proceeding just for us but I don't remember realizing that. I do remember thinking about the irony of the university trying to force protesting students, many on financial aid, to pay a $2,000 fine, we talked about that a lot.

After that arrest, I would go to SAMA meetings every day. Sometimes there were several meetings in one day, usually instead of class, which made sense because this was where I was learning everything, everything I wanted to learn. Two other first-year students and I wrote a seventeen-page document for the SAMA press kit about how need-aware was a racist and classist policy. Since we were at Brown, our struggle became national news—the *Washington Post* did a story a few days later, CNN came to campus, we were trying to get Jesse Jackson to support us.

The university denounced us, they called us violent, they continued to press charges. At one point, the new president of the university agreed to meet with us, or twelve of us who represented the steering committee. Or maybe we were the steering committee. Now I don't believe in steering committees, but I didn't know that yet. Anyway, we met with the president, and it was eerie because he knew all of our names before we introduced ourselves; he came right up to me and said hi Matt, not even Matthew like on my registration, shook my hand and looked me in the eyes. We'd smuggled in a tape recorder because we knew he would lie and we wanted proof. At some point the tape ended and there was a click—I don't know how he knew this meant we had a tape recorder. Thinking about it now I guess he probably knew in the same way that he knew our names ahead of time. Anyway, he became enraged and the meeting ended.

And then one week after our University Hall occupation the Rodney King verdict was announced; there was a forum in one of the largest halls on campus, right next to University Hall. You know what they say about kids in ivory tower institutions living in a bubble, we had that conversation a lot—that's what kids in ivory tower institutions like to talk about. I didn't think I was living in a bubble, that's for sure. But there I was helping to forge a struggle for racial and economic justice, and I didn't even know the Rodney King verdict was about to take place. I'm not even sure I remembered who Rodney King was. For weeks beforehand I'd flyered for the upcoming SAMA action, talking to mostly blank faces about the importance of "need-blind" admissions, and then those four LAPD officers were acquitted for the beating of Rodney King, the famous video broadcast across the country yet somehow they were still not guilty. For days, people rioted, especially in LA, and I remember going downtown to join the protest in Providence, and then back to organize more SAMA actions.

Our University Hall takeover was the culmination of several years of activism on the part of students, including a 164-page report presented to the administration the year before, involving research, analysis, and recommendations—students were doing the university's job. And paying the university at the same time—what a racket. We sent out press releases and held press conferences and went flyering and tabled and made banners and signs and held pickets and organized another big demo where we planned to encircle University Hall. We got faculty and administrators involved and contacted other schools protesting for equal access in Rhode Island and across the country, and I even kind of remember a march through downtown. What did it lead to, all this struggle—years of struggle, really? Nothing, that's what it led to. Not a single structural change at the university. And that's where I learned the most.

Elyse and I also learned a lot from taking ecstasy that was actually acid, although I wouldn't find out it was acid until years later. Kayti sent it to me—she said it was Joy, ecstasy in tab form, pure MDMA, and it was joy the way you could see the structure of things, the structure you were trying to escape. One time Elyse and I walked by one of those emergency fire alarm things and it fell over, crashed to the sidewalk, no alarm and were there really sparks? Another time we were gliding above the ground and we made up songs for the cars: Don't run us over, that's bad, because then we would be dead, and that's sad. Sad was one of the ways we connected, we could finally say it—every day was another opportunity to break down, and to break down the breaking down, and this didn't necessarily feel hopeful but it felt, we felt, we were feeling.

Of course, we felt trapped in different ways. Late at night on weekends, we would often end up at Dunkin' Donuts, after whatever party ended and we were still high. We smoked a lot of pot: it made us crazy and we loved that, we loved being crazy so late at night we'd end up at Dunkin' Donuts. I was eating things I would never eat if I wasn't high—I'd outgrown anorexia but I was still frightened by fat, what could be worse than donuts although they had muffins too, I tried to stay with muffins. And we would smoke pot in the back of Dunkin' Donuts. Sometimes we would pass out there, and in the morning people would come looking for us, our friends.

If we left before morning, tripping over ourselves and I would start to feel disgusting, back in my body the way I usually felt out of my body. I would hurl the donuts or muffins into the street and I remember Elyse was stunned that I would throw something away like that, something you could eat. I don't think she told me, not right then. She was spending more on books than her mother had for food. Once her mother sent her a rug, a woven Guatemalan rug in the style that was very popular at the time for frat boys who drank Cuervo and wore ponchos, a gesture of care, and I took one look at it and said: That's tacky. I might've even said: Get rid of it. Or, if I didn't say that, it's what I meant.

When I'd first arrived at Brown, I felt a social ease that I'd never experienced before—this was one of the things that gave me a certain kind of status. Or maybe it was the other way around, sudden social status gave me a certain kind of ease? At first I felt an intoxication from this shift, but then I began to feel like I was inhabiting a role that represented everything I'd always wanted to challenge. Elyse and I were becoming an item for the disaffected kids on campus, the ones with dyed hair who studied semiotics, older students, they saw our confidence and came right up to befriend us, bring us to parties where only upper-class students were invited. I mean upper-class as in older. We were the new item, a prize traded for avant-garde cachet: I'd never been that kind of item before and it made me feel grandiose and then emotionally dead.

Elyse and I would talk about who was crazy and who was insane, crazy was good but insane was even better. One night Elyse saw the world in blocks, she was surrounded by blocks, fetal position on the ground her eyes in permanent panic from a Robitussin high. When we were on mushrooms, I got scared because Elyse was on a different level of reality, I wanted her to come back to this level but she kept changing her sweatshirt and her expression. You keep on changing, I will not know who you are—Elyse left a note: Death is room temperature.

Maybe that was it—we were finally finding a place where we could be dramatic and then talk about it: my body felt like broken shards, I was ruining my life to beat my parents on their terms, I'd come to Brown to look for activism and instead there was so much apathy, why were people so apathetic? And scheming—everyone was scheming, like there was some high-stakes game to find it, find it now, it was me, us, have you tried this yet? Try it. Everything in my life had been leading up to this point.

I grew up believing that I was evil, that if anyone ever saw my true self they would know I was a monster that deserved to die. And I didn't want to die, except when I wanted to die, but I didn't want to know that and so I knew that I always had to hide everything. I had to hide everything so they wouldn't know.

They were parents and teachers and kids at school—grandparents too, and everyone else I might encounter. I wanted them to think I was perfect. Since I always did well in school it was always assumed that I would go to a good college, I mean that was assumed for everyone in my school, but some of us would go to college, and some of us would excel, and I was one of the kids who everyone believed would always excel.

This was childhood: I needed to do better, better than my father—he went to Oberlin, medical school, became a psychiatrist, a psychotherapist—I had to go to a more prestigious school, become more successful, buy a bigger house, make more money; this was the only chance I had, the only chance not to die. Except then I started to realize that was death too. That's when I knew I was trapped.

THE END OF SAN FRANCISCO

When Elyse and I were getting ready to move to San Francisco, my favorite song went, "I live for drugs, I live for drugs, I live for drugs—and it's great." Thrill Kill Cult with those industrial beats and campy at the same time, and sure, there was that time when I called myself on the phone to ask: Where are you? Or worse, when the dealer laced the mushrooms with something that turned my body into knots of pain and Elyse was massaging my back to try to help but all I could think about was the ambulance, I hope she calls an ambulance. There were the times when Elyse would go deep inside almost fetal and I'd be flailing, but even those times felt like living, which is learning anyway.

Crystal was different—just a bump or two and you'd be in the sky dancing until whenever, until forever, until the crash. That was the problem: the crash. Like your whole body was splitting apart and you would never feel anything again but this sadness and pain. Day after day of thinking about it, maybe just a bump, it's all you could think about but you didn't want to do more, more meant there would be nothing else.

Did I really do a bump before bed, on the worst nights in that apartment in the Inner Richmond, the one we rented after our first two months in San Francisco, but before we found what we really wanted? If we ever did. Elyse, did we ever find what we wanted? I know I found activism and ACT UP and sex that finally felt like dreaming, and of course more hair dye and shoplifting collaborations and industrial clubs and house clubs and even the club where activism and dreams came together, but I also found crystal, maybe once or twice a week but a few times a week meant that everything else was the crash. A bump before bed, just so I could feel pleasure.

This was one of the things that split us apart, Elyse and me. We were used to breakdowns, we broke down every day. We celebrated it, called ourselves crazy, manic, insane. We both knew by now that everything wasn't as simple as we'd thought it would be, back when we'd read that article in *Rolling Stone* or maybe it was *Spin* about how you could make $45 an hour doing phone sex, but then Elyse ended up making about $8 an hour and I don't think I ever made much more than $8 a day. We were working for different lines, hers was the standard straight woman deal and I worked Dial-a-Daddy and Lola's Line. We both got on general assistance and food stamps, which was actually enough to live on since our rent was cheap enough and we added in a bunch of other scams. Elyse had grown up on welfare but for me it was a way to get by without giving in, at least until they took it away and then I would figure out something else. After a while, Elyse got a data entry job at a software company in Berkeley.

Elyse and I were used to breakdowns, but this breakdown

with crystal wasn't something we could celebrate. Especially when we weren't doing it together, so we'd fall apart separately and then it would be time to do laundry or get groceries, those mundane tasks that had bonded us before but now maybe I'd be on day three without crystal and Elyse would have just crashed or the other way around. This was when we started letting each other down.

I had this idea that Elyse and I would collect pint glasses from all the cafés we went to, and when we were arguing we would throw them out the window and listen to them shatter. To try to defuse the tension. But still there was the tension. We'd grown into this relationship that we thought meant always, but always was hard to manage when we hadn't quite grown away from what we'd fled, childhood and everything we were supposed to be.

For me, critique meant love, it was the same thing—if I really loved someone I would tell them everything I was thinking, that meant respect. That's what I'd grown up with: it was the Ivy League that I was fleeing, it was my father's rage, it was how I'd survived. I'd figured out how to make my own rage political, to wield it as a tool for analysis and instigation. I knew how to remain calm no matter what in activist settings, but in my intimate relationships this was more difficult to manage.

Elyse had this pattern where she would subsume her identity to the other person, the person who she loved, me, and I didn't yet know how to see that pattern and break it. I'd always wanted to inspire self-expression at any cost, yet there was also a way in which my place in the world with Elyse, our place as a different kind of unit felt so charged. One of the things about Elyse and me, one of the things that was different from any relationship I'd had before, was the physical comfort. Not just the breakdowns magnified by drugs or the drama of figuring everything out, but that comfort: it's what held us together. And held us. There was something about the two of us entering a room, the way we could create safety by unwinding the boldness inside. When Elyse and I moved into our apartment in the Mission, it was the beginning of all our dreams coming together except our dreams together were already coming apart. That's the best time for dreams.

But now I'm not talking about Elyse and me anymore, or not just Elyse and me, but a whole generation of queers who came to San Francisco to try and cope. We were scarred and broken and brutalized but determined to create something else, something we could live with, something we could call home or healing or even just help, I need help here, can you help? We were incest survivors, dropouts, whores, runaways, vegans, anarchists, drug addicts, sluts, activists, and freaks trying not to disappear. We paraded down the streets in bold and ragged clothes too big or too small, we shared thrift-store treasures and recipes and strategies for getting day-glo hair color to last. We exchanged books and zines and flyers and gossip, got in dramatic fights over politics, over the weather, over clothing, over who was sleeping with whom—we held each other, we painted each other's nails and we broke down, honey we broke down.

We were the first generation of queers to grow up knowing that desire meant AIDS meant death, and so it made sense that when we got away from the other death, the one that meant marriage and a house in the suburbs, a lifetime of brutality both interior and exterior and call this success or keep trying, keep trying for more brutality, but when we got away it made sense that everywhere people were dying of AIDS and drug addiction and suicide because we had always imagined death. Some of the dead were among us, just like us, just trying to survive. Others were more in the distance, the elders we barely got to know except as we lost them. We went crazy and cried a lot, or went crazy and stopped crying, or just went crazy.

We believed it was us against them: they were straight people, they were abusers, they were rapists and landlords and cops, they were parents and politicians and anyone with designer clothes. They were the gay people who congregated in the Castro—apathetic, straight-acting gay men who went to the gym and dressed like clones in white t-shirts and baseball caps, gay men who hated women and fat people and people of color and sissies and anyone who was different, really, and we were different—we were absolutely certain of that.

We were vicious and vibrant, we judged with a purity that can only be imagined when you're really imagining. We held elaborate conversations, debates really, about when and where it was appropriate to shoplift. Some of us thought anywhere was okay, because the actual crime was the selling and marketing. Unless we had control over it, and were selling something like time with the bodies we were learning to call home: sex work didn't feel like shopping, at least not for us because we were the ones selling. Sometimes you worked under some boss with sex work too, and then it was just as exploitative—they stole from us, but usually we got paid better than at a coffeehouse, although it changed us too, and that wasn't always a good thing.

Some of us thought you could steal from chain stores, but not independent stores. Some of us decided that anything posh made a legitimate target, or anywhere that sold meat, or maybe someone we knew got fired so that meant we had free rein and even insider tips. But it's also true that people ended friendships when they thought someone was getting carried away, not carried away in the glamorous way, like when you walked into a store with a friend and carried a futon outside to your car and drove off—that made you a legend. But if you started stealing from your friends, you were becoming someone to avoid.

One of the most popular posters at the time was the one that said I Don't Think I'm Going to Work Today—I Don't Think I'll Go to Work Tomorrow. Your Body Is a Battleground was everywhere too. My favorites were the Homocult posters: Give Us Your Children—What We Can't Fuck, We Eat. And: Bent Fucker—Stolen Bent Cheap Filth. Most people thought the best job was welfare if you could still afford your rent, even better if you proved yourself crazy and got SSI because that was permanent although those of us who got arrested doing civil disobedience were worried about SSI because we thought it would make it easier for them to put us away. Maybe it was okay to work at somewhere dead-end that could still be used as a resource, like a copy shop. A corporate job could be overlooked, as long as you didn't care about it and you brought home free office supplies and complained all the time and then maybe you eventually became a stripper, or you became a stripper while you were still working at the corporate job. But if you started moving up at the corporate job, beyond something like data entry or telemarketing, then you might be getting suspicious. Although if you grew up on welfare, that was different— even moving up at a corporate job wasn't necessarily suspect. The worst thing anyone could say about someone was that they might have a trust fund: that meant they couldn't be trusted. No, the worst thing anyone could say was that you were a rapist, a rapist with a trust fund.

We argued about revolution—most of us thought it was the stupidest thing we'd ever heard of, you'd just take power and oppress everyone else, right? But then there were the ones who believed we were the stupid ones because we didn't believe.

We argued about drugs—drinking and pot were always okay, unless you started flaking out and couldn't leave the house, and some of us liked all drugs, the more the better, but then others liked everything except crystal and heroin, or everything except heroin. Most people thought heroin meant you would eventually steal from your friends, which was almost as bad as having a trust fund. Coke wasn't around, even though I was always looking.

Some of us were vegans—we were trying not to participate in any form of animal cruelty, and we looked at everyone else like they didn't have enough courage. Some of us believed in activism more than anything, sometimes even more than we believed in our friends, our friends who weren't activists, but then some of us thought activism was stupid, you would never get anywhere, you must have a trust fund if that's what you believed in. We were all sluts, or if we weren't sluts then we were trying to be sluts, and if we weren't trying to be sluts then we were talking about sexual abuse although we could also talk about sexual abuse and sluttiness, the two together, and we knew that made us stronger.

Obviously we believed in attitude: if someone said something about not wanting to judge people, that was New Age garbage. New Age garbage was almost as bad as a trust fund, it was the same thing as stealing from your friends because you were stealing their rage. There was good drama and bad drama, but there was always drama and this didn't necessarily feel uncomfortable because we had always known drama.

I'm talking about us, because that's what we believed. We thought we were creating our own system of understanding, our own values, our own way of challenging the status quo. I don't know if I'll ever believe again, and that's why I'm writing this. I don't go to the Mission now, or I try not to go, or if I do go then I go in a different way. Not just because of the party-ing suburbanites who live there now. They live everywhere. We were once partying suburbanites too, many of us, but we came to San Francisco to escape. There are still people who come for the same reasons, but they don't find what they're looking for, or what I was looking for, or if they do find it then I still can't believe.

Some of us had grown up rich and more of us poor, but we could see the way that queer freaks and artists and activists made the Mission a safer place for the yuppies we despised. We dyed our hair crazy colors and pierced and tattooed whatever we could think of, but still we were mostly white and young and hip, even if we would have denied the young and hip part. We brought the trendy restaurants and boutiques that we stared at with anguish and disgust, the yuppies we scorned—it was our fault that the Mission was no longer known primarily as a high-crime Latino neighborhood or just a place for thugs and welfare cheats and crack addicts on disability. We were the beginning of the end and we didn't know what to do because we'd just found the beginning.

When Elyse and I moved into our own apartment in the Mission, we found a place one block from ACT UP meetings, two blocks from Junk, three blocks from Rainbow Grocery—most of our friends lived within ten blocks, and the rest of them wanted to. Someone was always having a potluck, or an activist meeting, and if there wasn't a potluck or a meeting then maybe margaritas at La Rondalla or some party where every-one would argue, or try not to argue but get in fights anyway. Even in our kitchen, sometimes there were different allegianc-es and we argued about that too, it felt important to argue, to figure everything out.

This was when I went to DC for the March on Washington, a spectacle of assimilation if there ever was the one, but also I met Zee, we slept together and then got arrested together, what could be more romantic? And then we got bashed and already we were taking care of one another. Soon he moved to San Francisco to join me, although we didn't call it that. He said he was already planning to move to San Francisco.

When Zee arrived, I was in the middle of a two-week dance intensive, getting up in the morning to do contact improvisation all day and then afterwards I was worn out and drained but there was something else there, my body and this boyfriend, our bodies and there was the way he held me but mostly his eyes, they would always get glossy when he looked at me, even when we were fighting, which happened pretty soon but what happened sooner was that I remembered I was sexually abused. Zee was telling me about a professor who raped him and I was holding him but thinking why can't I feel it or actually I went past the not-feeling to thinking why, why get so upset about something like that, it's happened to me hundreds of times.

I was looking at the outline of Zee's face and there was an extra dimension, everything was moving diagonally upwards and back. Not just a physical dimension but an emotional dimension of terror. I shut my eyes and saw a cylindrical blue metal tunnel like my grandmother's laundry chute to fall into and get out of the house but it was floating, shifting angles. Layers of fluorescent dots in chains: blue, lavender, green. Remembering when I was a kid and I couldn't sleep because of the dots, I thought it had something to do with the way I shut my eyes too tightly. I'd wake up screaming and my mother would soothe me back to sleep. I'd see faces in the navy blanket, eyes on my walls and the same terror, like something horrible was going to happen and there was nothing I could do. I used to think the dots related to atoms, that somehow I could see the structure of things. Afraid of the dark, keep my entire body covered, even my head, run for the light in terror if I need to get up.

Everything in the room was flickering and shaking, no stillness except for my body. I was crying like I did when I was four, I could feel it was exactly the same. I wrote: Is it something to do with my father, his naked body? Just that sentence, I mean that sentence among everything else, everything else I was feeling. Zee knew what it meant, he'd already dated someone who'd been sexually abused. He saw it when there were places where I didn't want him to touch me, toward my neck or down my belly and I would freeze. I just thought that was sex: I leave, they can have fun. No one had ever noticed before.

How lucky to live in this house in the Mission, in a culture that talked about rape, a culture where we could go crazy and it was okay, it made sense, sometimes it was the only thing that made sense.

Most people didn't have living rooms in those days, I mean not most people we knew, so the kitchen was the center of our house—people would flow in and out and entire relationships would be negotiated and transformed over that table between the curving sofa and the chairs we borrowed from a laundromat. Like when Andy entered our house passing flawlessly as a clueless rich kid, asking a lot of questions. We didn't ask those kinds of questions, or if we did ask it was in a different way, a way that meant we'd always known. Andy came from Seattle as an official queer youth working for the American Friends Service Committee—in Seattle their project was the queer youth center, but we couldn't figure out what they were doing in San Francisco, other than giving Andy a place to live in an upscale neighborhood just above the Castro. When Andy started saying he was working class, everyone was appalled—who did he think he was kidding? When he dyed his hair blue, we thought he just looked like a prep with blue hair. When he said he wanted to be vegan, we smirked.

But we also listened. No, that's not true: I listened. I mean, it was Andy who first told me I needed to write my stories down. When I started turning tricks, I would tell these elaborate tales—like the one that started like this: It's my fifth trick, he calls around eleven, says do you go to Concord. I say 100 an hour, 250 for the night, wash up, catch the last train, and of course he isn't there. So I'm standing there waiting, thinking he's not going to show up and there isn't another train till morning and what the fuck am I gonna do. Finally this guy shows up in Speedos and a windbreaker, says are you Tyler, like there's anyone else around with pink hair. Then we're driving along, he's pushing my head to his crotch saying suck my cock suck my cock and I'm sucking his limp dick, he's doing Rush every few minutes and squeezing my balls and we're driving in the pitch dark—I don't know where the fuck we are.

I would tell these stories at the kitchen table, and Andy kept saying you need to write those stories down. A lot of people said that, but Andy was the most persistent. At the time I wrote poetry, so I wasn't interested. I thought the details of my tricks were too mundane—every hooker has stories, right? In my writing, I wanted to change language. But Andy said girl, you need to write those stories down, and then when I started to write them down I realized oh, these are good stories, I need to keep writing them.

I started turning tricks not long after I remembered I was sexually abused but I'd planned on it before. It made sense although I didn't necessarily know why, except that once I got to San Francisco I lived in a culture that made it possible. Not in that pathologized way of leaving my body: I knew that too well. I stayed conscious of when I would start to float up to the ceiling and then I'd focus on the pleasurable parts to bring myself back: the smoothness of skin, the intimacy of pressure, the feeling of his hand on the back of my head. I learned how to set boundaries using only my own movements as a guide. Sex work made it possible to live outside of convention and still make enough money to support myself. Sure, sometimes it could be depressing and draining, but not nearly as draining as some awful forty-hour job.

I always had friends in different realms, different worlds really—that's how it felt: the world of activism, which intersected but kind of didn't intersect with Mission dyke culture, and then there was that late-night club world, which didn't intersect with anything. Of course, we all lived between worlds, but most people didn't want to. One time I decided to have a big potluck and invite my friends from all these places, I wanted to see if I could connect them: I wanted to feel connected. It was a disaster—my activist friends were silent, my club friends rambled on about outfits or music or the weather or how vegan food was weird, everyone else just stared into space. One of my roommates who I rarely saw because he was in art school ended up getting smashed and chasing me down the stairs, grabbing me and trying to make out: I love you, I love you, he kept saying. Afterwards, people accused me of conducting a social experiment, a few of my activist friends in particular—I didn't try that again.

Elyse and I were still throwing pint glasses out the window in that Mission apartment where already it felt like we'd lived forever. Once we broke one of our downstairs neighbors' windows, but we didn't like them anyway—they were straight guys, and hippies too, or at least they had long stringy hair.

Camelia would get scared every time she heard those glasses shattering, but she never told us, and we never wondered. I want to say that we sat on that kitchen sofa and smoked, the way we tore down a piece of an anti-smoking billboard and put it in the bathroom as an ironic decoration, but the truth is that we didn't smoke in the house. We would walk through the laundry room attached to the kitchen and then across the back stairwell to the roof of the garage behind our building, where sometimes we'd see the landlord wandering around for no apparent reason. That was our smoking area, sometimes in the sun and sometimes in the dark, overlooking an alley that would later become famous for acceptable graffiti, an art project.

People smoked pot inside the house, mostly Elyse, since I didn't smoke much pot anymore. I thought it was boring. Elyse's dealer had a crush on her, so she would buy an eighth or a quarter and then he would give her a huge bag of shake, like a whole ounce. Once Elyse took that whole ounce and cooked up a batch of pot brownies—when we tried the first one it was disgusting, but then we got high and the brownies tasted better, we ate the whole batch in one sitting. We were high for three days and it was like we were back together again, together in hysterics.

I started becoming aware of the ways in which I wasn't so welcome in dyke spaces. I'd always noticed how sometimes I could become a fetish object, oh I like your hair your nails your pants your politics, and other times everyone would ignore me because I wasn't on the sexual menu, but I thought it was okay: I saw the way that dykes were treated in fag spaces. There was a certain kind of status I got from being one of the only fags welcome, or almost welcome, in dyke spaces—it meant I had done my work. But maybe it was time to question that type of inclusion, when it wasn't really inclusion.

Elyse kept planning to move out and get her own apartment, but then she would decide she didn't have enough money. So we would talk about who was going to move; we thought it would be better for our relationship. One time we went to a party at a new art space that was also someone's house—this was a different crowd, a newer crowd in the Mission, more money or maybe just attitude like money or college but some of the same people too, and this one person who was known for walking her slave around on a leash came up to me in the courtyard out back and said: Do you mind if I piss here? Sure, no problem, I said, and she pulled down her pants and pissed all over my legs, or mostly on my boots but on my legs too and I knew this game. I knew this game even though I'd never played it, never played it in this way but I stood there and acted like I didn't even notice. Kind of like when someone called me faggot on the street, except then I might wave and say hi.

Afterwards I felt so distant, shaking a little bit like childhood but enraged too, and this was one of the things we talked about in the kitchen, how S/M was becoming so trendy and whether, when something becomes really trendy, it can only go wrong. Sure, we were also angry about plaid pants on the runways, fashion victims who dyed their hair with Manic Panic, and mainstream gay men who wore combat boots, but this was different because it wasn't just a fashion choice. Kind of like how I never wanted to recommend turning tricks to anyone, because of how it would change your life—I would share all my knowledge but I never said do it, you should do it, it's easy, like a lot of people said.

Earlier I said something about how New Age was just above trust fund trash in the hierarchy of morals, although the truth is that this was the West Coast, so you'd go to a party, any party, and someone would be sitting in a corner with a tarot deck. Sometimes even in our kitchen, and I was aghast at the lack of critical engagement but tarot was everywhere so eventually I learned to act like it was okay. Same with altars—it seemed like everyone in San Francisco had an altar, sometimes it was a bunch of Eastern religious symbols, take your pick and presto, instant meaning, but other times it might just be an empty cigarette pack from your ex-boyfriend, a yellowing black-and-white picture of a city from your dreams, twigs from the street after a big storm, a rock from the beach, and a few club flyers—and then it might become beautiful.

A lot of people had boundary issues—Zee would put his arms around Elyse to cuddle, and she would cringe. Actually, I cringed too—what was Zee doing? Soon we were breaking up and getting back together—we would stand on the side-walk for hours in tense conversation, maybe we were outside because I was smoking or on the verge of doing crystal again and Zee might have been stoned or pretending not to be, or one of us was trying to run away or something was stuck, I guess we were stuck.

Actually we were stuck right away, when Zee moved to San Francisco and was sharing my room and I would go out to that dance workshop and when I got home he hadn't gone anywhere. He wanted to get groceries—Rainbow was only a few blocks away, but he was worried he'd get lost. He'd grown up in a small town in Michigan and I didn't understand.

We fought because he would use words like "nature." I would say: What do you mean by nature? The grass, the trees, the cement, the buildings? Nature doesn't mean anything. We fought when he would disappear into a new affair and then I wouldn't hear from him for days—neither of us was interested in monogamy but it was hard for me not to know what was going on. I just wanted him to tell me although I'm not sure he knew how. He was worried I'd get jealous but really I got jealous because he didn't tell me. But then we would hold each other and there was so much in this physical intimacy—even if we couldn't figure out the rest then at least we could rest, I mean when we weren't fighting.

During one argument I got so frustrated that I threw something against Zee's wall and it scared him—I didn't understand because I wasn't throwing it at him but then I understood. One night on the street I started screaming because someone was coming after me in the dark but it was Zee, coming out to hold me or maybe not originally to hold me but then he was holding me. I wasn't afraid of him, I was afraid of my father, under the bed with an axe, hiding behind the curtains, he was still there.

At one point I decided I needed to take a break from sex because my body felt too distant with all the incest flashbacks and right then Zee called me to be in a porn video with him. We were always planning to do sex work together but then Zee would change his mind, something about how it would alter our relationship and now I'm sure he was right. He called me because his costar showed up strung out on crystal so they had to send him away, and I took his place because I needed the money, I'd just gotten fired from the used clothing store.

It was always difficult for me to get fucked, but more difficult on camera when they kept making us stop and start again, the painful part and then I couldn't come and Zee got angry because that meant we would have to go back. He didn't even hold me afterwards.

We kept breaking up, or almost breaking up, which was kind of the same thing, and my relationship with Elyse now felt more like a cause of stress than a respite—we would still do that thing where the whole world would become our eyes into eyes holding steady, but now usually one of us wasn't looking. I decided to go to Seattle. Just for a month, to take some space and figure out what to do. JoAnne was in Seattle—we hadn't stayed in touch since the March on Washington but Garrett had her number.

Garrett was someone who I definitely didn't trust. He would follow people around, mostly dykes, first it was Angie who was one of Elyse's friends, and then it was Elyse, and Elyse told me I was being judgmental because I said I didn't like the way Garrett would become whoever he was around. We'd had this conversation before—who the fuck wasn't judging everyone all the time, that's what I wondered.

But now Elyse and I were in a place where we didn't always know our relationship would survive, and it's true that I would take one look at certain people and make pronouncements: She just wants to be friends with you because she doesn't have any sense of self. He's a pathological liar. She's using you. He's just another clueless rich kid. She's a hipster.

Hipsters were the enemy—we all agreed about that. They were vapid culture vultures who didn't have any politics. They looked kind of like us, so we had to constantly draw the boundaries. We were always talking about how hipsters were taking over, soon there wouldn't be anyone but hipsters in the Mission. Why did you invite that hipster over to your house? I can't believe you went to that hipster bar. We went to that party, and it was nothing but hipsters, so we grabbed a few drinks and then turned right back around.

We all cultivated critique—we were dogmatic in our alliances, self-righteous in our beliefs. But the broader Mission dyke culture that we called queer, so much of it was about loyalty at any cost. Loyalty could mean safety but it could also mean reenacting high school popularity contests and taking on the victors' roles. High school was only a few years in the past for most of us, even if we might have been scandalized if anyone had mentioned that. Accountability only occurred when people would get in dramatic fights, and it was more about whose team was stronger or more popular than about what actually happened.

I went to Seattle to get away—for a month, anyway, to figure things out. My two biggest relationships were falling apart, and maybe also my relationship with the queer cultures I thought were sustaining me. I met JoAnne at Caffe Paradiso and right away we were talking about sexual abuse and rape and crystal and how we were trying not to feel destroyed and maybe it was finally working. And then I spent a month in her room, we shared a bed and it never felt crowded. How could that be possible, that's what I'm wondering now, now when I can't sleep without everything arranged in the right way and then something always goes wrong anyway. But that was a different time.

I would go to the café during the day to read *The Courage to Heal* while JoAnne went to her phone sex job. She worked in an office with other women and office dividers—they were paid a wage instead of just commission, but it was only eight dollars an hour. When JoAnne got home from work, we would cook dinner or sometimes I would've already cooked, huge stir-fries with ginger and a homemade peanut sauce or if JoAnne was cooking then she used dill and cashews, and there was this way that we held each other and we held each other's rage, that was the key, the key that made us us.

Seattle was different from San Francisco—most people were actually from Seattle, or somewhere in the general region. The whole city felt suburban—even the neighborhood that white people were afraid of felt middle class. The counterculture kids looked like they bought their clothes at the mall—there actually was a counterculture mall with tiny stores that sold things like piercing needles and tattoos and I Can't Even Think Straight T-shirts. The apartment building where JoAnne lived was on a major street but it looked like something you would find on a suburban cul-de-sac, with blue prefab townhome-style apartments arranged around a parking lot.

In Seattle, people would get in blowout fights about which café served the best coffee. And people would get dressed up to go to cafés, I mean like they were going to a club, especially goth kids and ravers, and goth ravers—these were kids who couldn't get into most clubs yet, since Seattle was strict about IDs. There were cafés that stayed open until 4:00 a.m., and you could hang out all day and night without buying anything— that's because Seattle actually had a youth culture: youth need somewhere to go.

A few times, JoAnne and I went to Lambert House, the queer youth center, for dinner, and I was impressed—there were thirteen-year-old drag queens practicing runway, dykes with facial piercings who talked about running away, kids who would show up with bruises on their faces, covered up with makeup, and brag about all the clothes their parents were going to buy them. Once I saw this butch, clean-cut gay boy burst into tears because his parents were forcing him to join the military—he already looked like he was in the military, until he started crying. His parents showed up in a big white station wagon and he got in.

The strangest thing was that in Seattle I actually felt calm. People had always told me to relax—whenever someone said that I felt like they were telling me to die, right then, just die. I thought about staying in Seattle but I didn't want to be running away. At one point Elyse called and told me one of our roommates had decided to move out, I can't remember who it was because there was one room where someone was always moving out, and Elyse asked what I thought about inviting Garrett to move in. I said no way in hell, but do whatever you want.

And when I got back, Garrett had moved in—that's how Elyse and I were getting along. When I went into my bedroom, there was melted candle wax on the sofa. Garrett said oh, that's wax Zee poured on someone at the party, they were having sex and it was part of the scene. He said "scene" like he wanted to make sure I knew he was there—sometimes he looked like a six-foot-tall six-year-old who'd gotten into his punk-rock mother's Manic Panic stash.

I felt like the sofa wasn't mine anymore, it was some awful thing invading my room, so I lifted it up and tried to push it out the window. The window was big but still the sofa wouldn't fit. So I dragged it downstairs and outside to the street. Everything was tense and then Elyse decided to leave, maybe our relationship was over.

Elyse moved in with Angie, who was starting to wield a lot of power in our little world—she would hold court at parties with her tarot cards, telling people what to do, she saw it in the cards. Angie was tiny and always wired—it didn't matter whether she was yelling or whispering, she knew how to make it a big deal. She wrote poems that were like rants and when someone she liked performed at an open mic or at someone's house or showed their art at the dyke café where everyone went for coffee and drama, Angie would say: That was amazing. Sometimes it was amazing, but sometimes it was awful—soon there was this group of dykes who followed Angie around, they were constantly congratulating each other on bad art and bad relationships and bad behavior that they thought was truly amazing.

When Elyse moved out, Angie decided I was abusive, so that's what her followers decided too. I didn't know exactly what Elyse thought, because we weren't speaking, but I felt like she had a right to be as angry as she wanted. But Angie and I barely even knew each other.

The strange thing was that Garrett and I ended up becoming close, we would sit in each other's rooms and talk about incest flashbacks and desire and our fathers and the masculinity we were horrified by—we talked about consent, and whether it was really possible. Garrett couldn't believe I rarely got fucked, and I couldn't believe he thought getting fucked was the only radical choice. We got arrested for writing anti-police graffiti on a bus shelter—the ad showed a stick-figure drawing with a gun, shooting at other stick figures, black lines on a white background: "Children Draw What They See, and What They See Is a Crime." We made a necessary alteration, labeling the stick figure with a gun as a cop and the victims as unarmed people of color, and then we went to a nearby café.

It turned out that some store owner called the cops, and since Garrett and I both had brightly colored hair we were easily identifiable: we ended up in jail for almost two nights, first in a holding cell by ourselves, once they decided we had sugar in our pants, that's how they put it. I was grateful for that sugar once I took a look at the other holding cell, everyone arranged on top of one another, there was a fight and someone started screaming and the cops ignored it.

After a night in a blank room with those oppressive pale green walls, we ended up in the queen tank, where everyone assumed we'd gotten arrested for prostitution—I stayed awake while Garrett dozed; some guy in office clothes was screaming on the phone to his lawyer, he was the only one with a lawyer. Eventually the cops took Garrett and me to separate interrogations where they tried to get each of us to say the other one was the problem. We ended up with time served and forty hours of community service.

Maybe that's when we really bonded. Garrett made these day-glo stickers that everyone in our house loved, single words like WHORE or FREAK or VEGAN or DYKE or FAG or QUEER or something more complicated like QUEER VEGAN INCEST SURVIVOR. Garrett's favorite sticker said TRASH because that's what people had always told him he was, white trash but this was when white trash parties were really popular in the Mission among people who hadn't actually grown up white trash. These were the people who had grown up kind of like me and so I avoided them, not just because of their white trash parties but because I thought they would never know anything I wanted to learn. At the kitchen table, we would talk angrily about those parties, not just the fetishism but the emphasis on whiteness.

I remember those nighttime walks through the Mission and underneath the highway, crossing into South of Market to go to Junk after it moved to the Stud and we all agreed it was over. But I guess it wasn't totally over, because we still went there. Now there were straight tourists looking for three-ways, since the club got written up in one of the papers. The first time I went to Junk after I got back from Seattle I was so worried about running into Zee and how would I feel and then he wasn't there and I could breathe. Until he was there, and I tried to talk to people and act like it was okay, I mean like I was okay but around their heads I was looking out for him until I was dancing and then it didn't matter no it still mattered but I could dance like it didn't matter and then eventually maybe it wouldn't.

I remember those conspiratorial walks, down dark streets

and past warehouses and how we were trying to prepare for whatever might take place: if you looked up at the sky it would frame us, that's what I'm thinking now. Sometimes we looked, and sometimes we didn't. I can picture Elyse first, with her shaved head and bleached white hair, twirling in the dark although really we were just walking. But sometimes walking can be twirling, inside. Then Garrett and Andy, since Andy had moved down to San Francisco while I was in Seattle. We met for a second in Seattle when I was with JoAnne, but we really met in my kitchen. And on those walks: gossip and nerves, trying to act nonchalant. Tall skinny fags and dykes with bodies. There were others who joined us too and then there was JoAnne once she'd moved down from Seattle, freshly emboldened by the nails she'd forced through her ears—hardware always made the best jewelry.

And Melissa, she liked house music too so sometimes we would go to Your Sister's House instead of Junk, just the two of us and then there wasn't any drama just dancing—Melissa would wonder if any of these women were dykes but if they were then we never found out. I met Melissa at ACT UP and then later we were the token queers in the activist group that got me to stop doing direct action for a while, the group where everyone started screaming at me because I thought we should operate by consensus. Or not everyone, but the two people with the most power, Ivy League graduates who knew how to fight to win. They were people of color in a group started by and for people of color, and there was an unspoken sense that I wasn't acting grateful enough that they'd invited me in.

Melissa was one of the people who agreed with me, but she didn't say anything at meetings. She was kind of like some of my childhood friends, so awkward that most people couldn't see her, but her analysis was deep and immediate. Like when she met Zee, and said: You know, he totally objectifies you. And I hadn't thought about it that way before, but she was right—sometimes I felt like his beautiful object, something bold to hold. Melissa was stuck at her parents house after dropping out of school—she went to Yale and it traumatized her in some of the same ways that Brown traumatized me, but she stayed longer and it got worse and she tried to kill herself. After she got out of the hospital, she stayed in New Haven because she liked her life there outside of Yale, but now she was back at her parents' house, scared of her father in the hallway and sometimes she would stay at my house, especially after Junk, because it was a long way back to her house in the Sunset. We would share my bed and I would try to encourage her to get away from her parents but there was something that meant she couldn't—she would look away when she was trying to say it, voice shaking and I knew.

Once JoAnne moved in, I would go to her room when I was scared of my father's eyes and then she started talking about the dirty old man she needed to picture in order to get off, there was no other way—she needed that dirty old man. She realized it was her father and we would hold each other in that way that meant it was okay if nothing was possible and it was okay if everything was possible and then it was just okay. We would sob together, really sob—Zee held me in that way too but then it would fall apart. With JoAnne it felt like always.

When JoAnne and I were done crying, we would paint each other's nails and soak our hands in ice water. We would help each other with hair dye, the hard-to-reach places in the back, and then we would get ready to go out. Or get ready not to go out—it didn't matter, we still had to get ready. Sometimes we would combine drugs that didn't quite feel like drugs—black beauties that JoAnne brought down from Canada that were supposed to be speed but they were so calm to us that we decided they were caffeine. Or we'd do ephedrine and Xanax, I still had a lot of Xanax from my father's medicine cabinet, samples from the company arranged in a big box. We snorted everything on a shard of an old mirror because that's the way we liked it best, we were avoiding the drugs that squeezed us too hard but still we wanted that burn. Then we'd go to La Rondalla for margaritas and the photo booth, was there a photo booth at La Rondalla? There was so much laughter as we would tumble around.

In the kitchen we would remind each other to breathe and to chew, we were trying to stay calm but we also celebrated mania—we held each other and made carrot juice with ginger and then honey, we would dissect the drama. The first person JoAnne took apart was Garrett, she couldn't deal with the way he wanted her to be his mother, that's what he wanted from all the dykes in his life and JoAnne thought it was oppressive. That's when Garrett was getting really depressed. I mean he was always depressed: we were all depressed and that was fine or not fine but it was a given. Now Garrett would come into the house and slam the door and I would try to get him to understand why JoAnne was angry but then he started slamming the door on me. After that, when Garrett would come into the house, JoAnne and I would stay in the kitchen and continue laughing and making carrot juice, maybe we'd even laugh a little louder.

I don't know who decided this first, but eventually it was Garrett and Angie and everyone around Angie who decided that I was evil, and that I had possessed JoAnne—it sounded just as ridiculous then as it does now, but it's really what they decided. JoAnne made these cards that looked kind of like tarot cards—they said things like, "I'm just another brainless woman." And, "Don't ask me, ask Matt." And then JoAnne made cardboard horns for me and I wrote 666 on my forehead with lipstick. And when they all came over to help Garrett move out, I sat in the kitchen smoking and hissing and staring them in the eyes like the demon they wanted me to be—yes, we must have smoked in the kitchen. JoAnne chased them down the stairs and screamed for the whole neighborhood: You think you're feminists, you're not fucking feminists, it's just misogyny turned the other way!

Another time, we both wrote 666 on our foreheads, and JoAnne taped her mouth shut with duct tape and we went over to the dyke café and handed out cards that said Val Valley Pep Squad. We were trying not to feel silenced—if they thought we were possessed, then why not show them possessed?

But I almost forgot the hardest part, I mean the hardest part for me. No, I didn't forget, I was just trying to figure out how to tell it. When Garrett moved out, he spray-painted the sidewalk in front of our door, huge letters that said MATT IS A RAPIST. When I first saw those words I stood there and stared and felt my whole body pull in.

I didn't know what to do except to call Elyse. I said: You won't believe what Garrett wrote on my doorstep. Here he was calling me a rapist, just because it was the worst thing he could say. But Elyse still refused to support me: now I knew our relationship was really over.

I didn't know if I would ever again believe in this thing called community. Even now, fifteen or almost sixteen years later, it's like I'm there again, I can hardly breathe. I'm on the phone with Andy, who says: I never realized all that affected you so much.

But it did, honey, it did.

At the time I still wanted to be invulnerable, or at least

to seem invulnerable, and so I channeled all my emotions into a politicized rage, rage at this culture that had made and betrayed me—what do you mean community? I dissected the betrayal, step by step. I went off on scenesterism, on followers, on the emptiness of Mission dyke posturing.

But I didn't talk about how I'd believed.

WIDE AWAKE

When JoAnne started doing heroin, it wasn't a big deal, or at least it didn't seem like a big deal. She would sit in her room on the rocking chair, eyes closed and I would ask: Are you sleeping? No, she would say— no, I'm wide awake.

What do you see?

Everything.

Then the next day we would go on making carrot juice and entertaining ourselves with the most scathing critiques of everyone we knew, and JoAnne would tell me: You really have to work at it, you have to work to get addicted. It's not like crystal, she would say. We both knew about crystal—you definitely didn't have to work to get addicted. Sometimes JoAnne would sit in her room on heroin and paint—she thought we should do it together, it would be fun. But I didn't want to make art on drugs. And I didn't understand why JoAnne was shooting heroin instead of snorting it. Heroin definitely wasn't the drug for me—I wanted to be on all the time, I didn't want to close my eyes and watch. I don't even know if I wanted to close my eyes.

Before Garrett moved out, back when we were still friends with Angie, or friendly at least, we all went over to Angie's office with a few of her friends who were maybe still our friends and made a zine together. Maybe Andy was there too, was Andy there? Elyse was probably at work. Angie worked at a nonprofit and she had the key to the office, where there was a photocopier. We each made a page in this zine and a lot of it was about rape and incest and sex work and rage and it's funny to think we made the zine right before we all became enemies, because at that moment it felt like we were finally getting along. Maybe that's why I ended up talking about Riot Grrrl when I started to write about this period in my life, even though Riot Grrrl never really meant anything to me: we were writing about rape and sex work and rage and then we were enemies.

Andy says: Yes I was there, I was there when we made that zine, it was called *The Mean Zine*, and you were supposed to write about the cruelest thing you had ever done to anyone. Me: That's a different zine, I don't think I was there for that one. Andy: Yes you were, we only went there once. I have that zine in storage.

Me: But I have it right here, and it's not called *The Mean Zine*. Andy: That's right—we made two zines. There was the other zine where I drew a diagram of a cock harness unfolded, and then I labeled it "The Day I Learned Codependency Was the Word on Valencia."

Me: I don't think that's what it says, maybe that was in the other zine. Andy: No, that's definitely what it says, because in *The Mean Zine* I wrote about throwing this boy out of a party in Seattle because he told me my boyfriend had cheated on me, and even though it was true I picked that boy up by the collar and dragged him out of the flat and down the hall and threw him out into the rain. And then I wouldn't let anyone let him back in, even though it wasn't my apartment.

Me: That's right, I remember that story, we talked about it in the kitchen, and you were still angry at that boy. Andy: But I felt terrible about it. Me: I know—that's why you wrote about it in *The Mean Zine*. But what did I write about? Andy: You did that stream-of-consciousness piece that was a list, like two cups of this and a teaspoon of that and I can't remember exactly what it said but then you said—add concrete.

Me: Oh, right—like a recipe. Andy: Yeah, like a recipe for cruelty—and everyone was stunned. And fawning, because you had just pulled that out and then it became the central piece in the zine. Even though the whole thing was a setup so that Ellen could write about that dinner party at your house, now they were all saying: That's amazing, you're amazing.

Me: Oh, right—Ellen wrote about how that dinner party where I invited people from the different parts of my life was the cruelest thing anyone had ever done to her—no wonder I don't remember that zine.

I'd decided to leave San Francisco sometime after I got back from Seattle, before or after Elyse moved out, I'm not sure. San Francisco was done for me, until JoAnne moved down. I probably wouldn't have decided to leave after she arrived. Except that I'd already decided.

I was pretty sure that leaving college was one of the best decisions I'd ever made, but I wanted to go back to Brown just to be certain, since I was getting ready to confront my father about sexually abusing me and I knew he wouldn't be paying for college after that. I'd left Brown three years before without completing my classes—I was doing activism instead. So now I figured I should try to get off academic probation, in case I ever wanted to finish college somewhere else. I planned to tell my father I would never speak to him again unless he could acknowledge sexually abusing me, raping me, molesting me, he could choose from these terms but I wanted him to acknowledge. I didn't think he would ever admit anything: maybe that's why he was a psychiatrist.

And I wanted to get away from what San Francisco had become, had become for me. In that apartment where I lived in the Mission with first Elyse and Camelia, and later JoAnne and Camelia and a lot of other people in between. It had become home because I finally felt it, felt it for the first time, felt. In that apartment where we lived on an alley called Sycamore, yes, my last name, but I was leaving anyway because I had already made up my mind.

When I got back to Brown, I was stunned: the people I remembered as alienated and quirky, weird and overwhelmed and expressive and dreamy, most of them had become pompous and disaffected, shuffling around abstractions in order to gain stature in the battle of ideas. When I had met them they'd just left the places where they'd grown up or whatever they called it, and now they were ready to leave again, graduate, they were ready and I was stunned at what they had become.

Looking back, I wonder if I had changed more than they had. But that's not what I thought then. In one of my classes there was this first-year with a barrette in his hair, awkward and alienated like the people I'd remembered, and I kept saying you need to get away, get away before this is what you become. And he left at the end of the year, moved to San Francisco, became a hooker and I didn't think that was a good choice for him because he always seemed out of his body, but anything was better than Brown. I would walk across campus as fast as I could, rush to my classes and rush away, and then second semester I decided I would live in Boston, that was the only way I could continue. I would drive down for class and then drive back—Boston was only an hour away, and I needed the distance.

In Boston someone was always playing the *Priscilla* soundtrack, I mean when they weren't watching the movie again. My room was right next to the living room so sometimes I would wake up to *Priscilla*, I couldn't think of anything worse. Except when someone was cooking bacon. Or playing Abba, which was also on the *Priscilla* soundtrack. My roommates even liked *To Wong Fu*, where Wesley Snipes, Patrick Swayze, and John Leguizamo play drag queens on a road trip—it was *Priscilla* relocated from the Australian outback to the US heartland. JoAnne would call me up and say: You know you're an addict, don't you? She was high, I could hear that hollow sound in her voice—kind of like Erin, the cokehead lesbian hairstylist with a bleached perm who we'd see at all the clubs in Boston, whenever she was really high all she could talk about was quitting: As soon as I finish this, I'm going to quit—do you want a bump?

Clubs had always been part of my life, but in Boston they became my life. Clubs and outfits—when my grandmothers came to Boston together to visit me I debuted my neon plaid tights, with contrasting polyester plaid cut-off shorts and a tiny plaid polyester shirt that somehow matched the colors of the clips in my neon hair and my grandmothers couldn't believe I wasn't doing this just to be provocative.

I showed them photo booth pictures from the clubs and they asked if I was a transvestite. I told them that language was outdated, only straight people said "transvestite." Do you wear dresses? When I'm in the mood.

Boston is where I got the name Mattilda. At first I was experimenting with Rhubarb, since that was the color of my hair, but when Gabby started calling me Mattilda it made more sense. When I met Gabby, she was this red ribbon fag who worked at the gay bookstore, but when I told her the red ribbon was just an empty symbol for straight celebrities to show they cared about their dying gay friends, she didn't get defensive. She'd only recently escaped a Christian fundamentalist cult that happened to be run by her father, but then a few months after I met her she became a tranny hooker club kid. I wasn't that into club kids, and sure I was a hooker but it was never something I recommended. But there's the way people see something about you and think it's what makes you who you are. It was my politics that helped me to create my own world but those politics were harder to understand than dressing up and going out and turning it out.

In Boston, you really needed to know how to walk. So let me tell you about runway: The point is that you walk like you're going to die right now you walk like you're never going to die you're never going to die as long as you keep walking and you walk like you're going to kill, kill with this walk and you walk like no one can touch you. And the truth is that no one can touch you, as long as you're walking. Well, maybe not the whole truth, but that's the truth in your eyes, which is the truth that matters, at least when you're walking.

And sure, you're also walking like a model, a model on those other runways, that's part of the turn, pose, but it's a different kind of model, at least the way I looked at it. Maybe a model for getting away, even if you're never going to get away you will get away on that runway.

When Andy visited me in Boston and we became close, one of the things he said was: You have to take responsibility for your influence. In Boston I was in gay worlds, not queer, I mean I was trying to make them queer but this was Boston, these were gay clubs, there were limitations. When the after-hours club would close we would get in my car and drive back and forth over the Mass. Ave. bridge and I would be way higher than everyone else because I was always trying not to do ecstasy so when I finally gave in it was later, in the middle of the after-hours club instead of at the beginning, and that's why the after-after-hours came to our house—I was so high I'd say come on, come over our house, everyone, and then we'd guide a caravan of queens crowded into cars through neighborhoods they were scared of.

But then after that was over, and Gabby and I were fighting with our roommates, the ones who got up at 6:00 a.m. instead of going to bed then, and I'd give my car keys to someone, anyone, I was too high to drive and high enough to get in the car with any other mess so we could float over the Mass. Ave. bridge as the sun was rising and then when we got to the end I'd say please, please can we drive over again.

Oh, but responsibility and influence. Andy meant this little world of club queens around me in Boston—maybe I'd inspired them to kind of not care about everyone who wanted us dead, we could create our own world instead. But then they believed too much in the drugs—drugs help you to not care. Except that wasn't the same thing as the critical distance I was trying to inspire, it was just distance.

In Boston, all the fags would make jokes about those trashy hookers on the block, dirty bitches giving everyone AIDS for five dollar no holler. But then wait, you'd be working the block and look, who's that over there? But then these other queens, the ones who weren't exactly queens before they met me and yes, I gave them a boost in that direction. Although if I wanted to encourage people to claim their own autonomy, how could I take responsibility?

Everywhere I went, people looked at me like they wanted to kill me. Sometimes they would tell me, they would tell me they wanted to kill me, and that's when I needed to walk. Like one time when Gabby and I were coming home from doing laundry, and this guy stopped his baby carriage and started screaming in our faces about his neighborhood and our faggot asses and how we better watch our backs and I wondered about that kid in the baby carriage. When someone dropped a cinderblock out their second-story window, and it fell down with a thud just a few steps in front of us, we kept walking.

In Boston, a good night would start with a few cocktails, continue with a hit of ecstasy, maybe a bump or two of coke while waiting for the ecstasy to kick in and then oh, that place up there above the ceiling and then Special K when you were falling, so you could sink into the ground, pot to bring back the floating, a Xanax to relax. When the drugs got really bad, it was the dealer's fault—the dealer gave us something awful. Like that batch of big flat tablets a yellow-brown color instead of white, there wasn't any ecstasy in that ecstasy. You would take the pill, and just when it started to kick in you had to rush to the bathroom to vomit—because of the heroin, that's what we thought, and then when the speed kicked in it would knock you over the head like the whole room was expanding and contracting at the same time. Everyone got used to that back and forth slam, and then when we got real ecstasy again people complained.

JoAnne was turning tricks on Capp Street, I can't remember when she started but Capp Street was the bottom of the line for hookers, why not take out an ad? JoAnne said she liked it on Capp Street, the girls watched out for each other, she wouldn't be able to turn tricks on her own. And I'm a fat dyke, she said, no one would call my ad. JoAnne was proud of being a fat dyke, she was just reading the marketplace. She would get in cars for $30 blow jobs, but it was so convenient—Capp Street was literally a block away from the house.

In Boston, sometimes I went to the boy block, usually it was empty but I did get my best trick there, the one who paid me the best, by the hour. We would always talk for at least two hours before doing anything else, but then during the sex part it was so hard for me not to freeze because of the way he touched me so soft and his body was all bones. I want to say that he was a crackhead, but actually I don't think there were drugs, I think he was dying. I liked the part where we talked about music, he would get all excited and even though it was classical music I would get excited too. The first time I worked the boy block, my friends got worried because I didn't come back for a while, they left me panicked notes on the parking meters.

Gay culture was scary, but I did appreciate the camaraderie. It wasn't so lonely at the clubs, waiting for the music to save me. Now Gabby and I would rush to the photo booth to get pictures of our outfits, at the big club that happened every Sunday, the highlight for Boston gay nightlife. Then I always went all the way to the back where I knew I would find the dancing freaks, but at the end of the night I would look for my friends so we could figure out the next stop.

JoAnne started taking care of one of her lovers who was kicking heroin, she'd hold her in all that shit and vomit and I can't remember what happened to that lover, I mean whether she got off heroin but then JoAnne was trying to kick. She sent me a book about recovery from drug addiction as a spiritual quest but I wasn't interested in spiritual quests. In the margins

JoAnne wrote: Considering my place on the social totem pole I'm rare to be alive at 21. And: Addicts are my teachers now.

JoAnne didn't want me to leave San Francisco, and I'm not sure I wanted to leave either—right at the moment when I was leaving it actually felt like home, at least in our kitchen, making stir-fries and dissecting everyone's drama. Afterwards, JoAnne tried to be friends with Angie again, or the people who were friends with Angie, or both, and I was never quite sure why, except it was hard to be a certain kind of dyke in the Mission unless you were friends with certain people. But now JoAnne was a junkie and the rule in the Mission was: A junkie will steal everything from you. It's not that they didn't talk to her, but they wouldn't let her in and I blamed them, blamed them for everything.

I always had rules for my addictions. I never did drugs during the day, unless I was still up from the night before. Every week I would stop for several days and everything would get much much worse unless we went out for cocktails, yes please, cocktails. Sometimes I would stop everything for a week or even a month, just to make sure I could do it, and everyone around me would be stunned and JoAnne would say: You know you're an addict, right?

JoAnne, I said, I know I'm an addict, but you're the one who's high right now—but you can come to Boston—we could get an apartment together, you'd be away from all your sources. But JoAnne insisted that I didn't want to see her this way. She moved back in with her mother, in the Seattle suburb where she grew up. Her mother wouldn't let her leave the house because she was worried she would get drugs, that was one of the rules for JoAnne staying there. I went to the corporate health food store in Boston and borrowed the largest size containers of all the fanciest vitamins and sent them to JoAnne. Her mother remembered that later: JoAnne really appreciated those vitamins, she said, she talked about you all the time.

But first, JoAnne's mother kicked her out, after JoAnne left the house and went to Seattle for the day. Soon JoAnne was back in San Francisco—Melissa was doing outreach on Capp Street when she ran into her. Melissa said: JoAnne doesn't look good. What does she look like, I asked. She's lost a lot of weight, and you can almost see through her skin. JoAnne called me to tell me about running into Vanessa on the street, JoAnne was spare-changing and Vanessa wouldn't give her any money but she told her she looked amazing.

JoAnne was so angry—Vanessa had never told her she looked amazing before, it was because of all the weight she'd lost. But I don't like where all this is leading—I want to tell you about the time JoAnne finally came to Boston, after Gabby and I moved into our own place and we had an empty room waiting. JoAnne loved the list I tacked up on the wall in the living room, actually it was all my daily lists taped together, maybe a month of them—various colors of scrap paper with tricks' names and numbers, grocery lists, and then certain things written over and over again like INCEST, because I was getting ready to confront my parents.

Sometimes JoAnne and I would stand in the living room and look at the lists—JoAnne would look at me like a professor, purse her lips and ask in an exaggerated parody of a British accent: Children, what are we going to talk about today? Then she'd wind her hand around in a circle with her pointer finger out like she was getting ready to read, Boston-queen-style, and boom, the finger would land right on INCEST. That's right, Professor JoAnne would say—Incest. Repeat after me: Incest. Spell that—I . . . N . . . C . . . E . . . S . . . T . . . Exactly—now, go home and tell your parents.

And then in New York, when Andy and I went to that party—it was a birthday party for Gregory, this boy who I had a crush on for at least a year, we were friends and there was all this sexual tension but I knew he was never going to sleep with me because I was a whore. That happened a lot in New York, not the crushes but the part where they wouldn't sleep with me once they found out what I did for a living. Even if we'd met in a backroom. Anyway, that night I was in an after-trick spending mood, so on the way to Gregory's house I thought I'd buy him a dozen roses, half yellow and half peach, but the person at the flower stand got confused and mixed two dozen together— oh well, I thought, I guess I'll give him two dozen. Globalization was hard at work providing roses for scarily cheap prices to East Village consumers like me. When I got to the party, I was embarrassed because Gregory's boyfriend had brought flowers too, but only three Gerbera daisies.

This was the party where at one point Gregory and three other fags were comparing Nikes—they were all wearing the same ones, and I said: That's enough to fund an entire sweatshop. Then one of them looked down at my boots, and said: Well, you're wearing a whole cow on your feet. I want to tell you about how JoAnne jumped in and said: Those boots are vegan! Then, on the way out, she somehow managed to stuff all the roses into her bag without anyone noticing—I should've bought them for her in the first place.

That was around the same time when my roommate's brother started staying in our apartment—we lived in an enormous commercial loft space in Williamsburg so there was plenty of room, but it was still annoying the way he literally pitched a tent in the middle of our apartment, and then he would bring home women to fuck and there weren't any walls and they would make all this ridiculously gendered hetero noise. I want to tell you about how JoAnne decided that if my roommate's brother had moved in without asking, she could move in too, so she got a bigger tent, and pitched it right next to his tent, and then when he and some new fling were fucking she started screaming along with them.

But back to Boston, when Gabby and I were selling K to save money so we could take the train cross-country and figure out where the hell to move—we needed to get out of Boston, that was for sure. But then, instead of saving money, Gabby ended up doing more drugs. So JoAnne ended up going with me instead, and I want to tell you about all our crazy adventures on the train, like when we snuck into an empty sleeper car and they caught us but not until after we'd slept and when we told them we couldn't afford to pay the difference they said we'd have to get off at the next stop. Luckily that was our stop: the Twin Cities on Halloween, where we didn't have anywhere to stay so we went to the big gay club where there were so many guys dressed up in military uniforms we kept counting—20, 21, 22—wait, did we already get that one? And then we ended up at the twenty-four-hour Denny's where we told our story to the queeny waiter with dyed hair who was kind of flirting with me and he gave us speed pills and told us we could wait until his shift ended, and stay with him.

But I can't tell you any of these stories because JoAnne was already dead. She never made it to Boston, or New York, and now I was going back to San Francisco so her parents wouldn't get her journals.

When JoAnne died, it was important for all of us to say that she didn't die an overdose. She died because the hospital refused her health care. She was kicking heroin and they admitted her, hooked her up to an IV for two days then said you don't have enough money to need us. She had active TB and a bladder infection. They gave her Tylenol. She couldn't walk. Her roommates carried her home. Later that night, they found her in the backyard, naked in the grass and laughing. The next day she was dead.

I don't know why it mattered so much for us to say she didn't die of an overdose: no matter what, the hospital killed her. I was stuck in Boston with nothing except Gabby and drugs, and I was trying not to do drugs. I'd just confronted my parents about sexually abusing me and it didn't feel like a release it just felt awful. That's when I got the call from Elyse saying JoAnne was dead, and I flew out to San Francisco the next day. I didn't know what else to do.

I'd known people who had died of AIDS—guys I'd slept with, activists I'd admired. Like Billy, who arranged candles around the bathtub the one time we had sex and maybe he was trying to make it romantic because he didn't know how long he had left. Or Colin, who I met at ACT UP, when he was sick he asked me for hair-dyeing tips and we laughed because it turned out he didn't need to use much bleach since his hair had already turned gray. I'd known people who had died of overdoses, people who had killed themselves, people who had disappeared and no one knew what happened, but none of these relationships ever felt permanent like my relationship with JoAnne—no matter how bad things got for either of us, I always thought JoAnne and I would create a life together.

San Francisco welcomed me like I was a widow and that's how I decided to move back. I returned to Boston to prepare, decided to take the train cross-country in a few months. In those days, you could buy one ticket and travel anywhere you wanted for thirty days, so I figured I'd spend some time in Minneapolis and Chicago and Seattle, just to see. A friend of JoAnne's lent me her one-bedroom apartment in Chicago and she went to stay with her girlfriend. I couldn't believe she had so much space, in a fancy neighborhood even—Chicago was way cheaper than San Francisco or Boston.

I went to Chicago for the music, the music that I lived for, that hard clanky knock-you-down after-hours magic. I needed something to distract me. The problem was, I didn't know where to find that music—it wasn't what they called the Chicago sound, deep and soulful, it was the new Chicago sound. But I found a place that looked right, from the description at least.

On my way I stopped at a bank machine, and maybe I noticed two guys in a car looking over at me like I didn't deserve to live, but this happened all the time. I realized I'd walked the wrong way, so I went back down the same street, a dark street really but I hadn't thought about it—that's when they jumped out of the car, from behind, one of them held a gun to my head and the other said give me all your money, so I did, but it was only twenty dollars. They said something like let's teach this faggot a lesson or maybe they didn't say anything but I knew.

First I remember thinking oh, scream, scream for help and so that's what I did, and then they hit me in the face with the gun, several times, and then slammed my head against a brick wall, and then they got in the car and drove away and there was blood everywhere, pouring down my face and onto my pink scarf and I remember thinking okay, at least I know where I am, I'm right by the apartment, I can get back, I'm right by the apartment. And then, once I got upstairs, I thought: Don't get blood on the carpet.

In the mirror everything was red, especially the pink scarf, and I didn't know what to do so I wiped off the blood with paper towels and got some ice for my face but there was too much to cover. I called Melissa in San Francisco, maybe because her roommate was a nurse or maybe I didn't remember that, but her roommate said: Mattilda should go to the hospital right away, with a head wound she might have a concussion. And then I remembered her roommate was from Chicago, so I said where should I go? And she said oh, she's in Chicago, don't go to the hospital—wait until tomorrow, and go to a clinic.

For the next week, when I walked around on the street with two black eyes and a swollen nose, people really stared. They wanted to know what happened. It kind of made me scared just to go outside, and I was worried the bruises wouldn't heal before I got to San Francisco: I always wanted to look amazing when I felt awful. But then, by the time I arrived in Seattle, where I stayed with Andy, it just looked like I had been crying a lot.

When I got back to San Francisco, I tried not to go to the Mission because it only felt like a loss. I was staying with Derek in the Haight: before I thought JoAnne was the only person I'd ever shared a bed with for a month, but now I remember I stayed with Derek in his bed for a month too. In a tiny room barely larger than the bed, he paid $150 for it and we split that for the month. It was kind of like we were lovers except we didn't have sex, we just talked about everything and slept with our arms or shoulders touching lips brushing against neck and sometimes Derek would wake up screaming in the middle of the night, sweat drenching the sheets and I would pet his head and say it's okay, it's okay. Just like when we first met—I guess it would be a while before I began to have trouble sleeping.

It's not like anything was okay, except in that bed with Derek where I felt so comfortable in my body, whole in the way I was trying to become, and I wondered if we should have sex because of the safety. But I didn't want to lose the safety.

I ran into Zee at a café in the Lower Haight—we hadn't

talked since I'd left San Francisco because he didn't want to talk and in Boston I had even thrown out the Cocteau Twins album that was always playing when we were fighting, *Heaven or Las Vegas*, was that our soundtrack? I ran into Zee and it was like suddenly we were friends again. We made plans to go with Derek to a bonfire on Corona Heights to watch the sunset, but then I got a trick so I couldn't go and Derek and Zee went alone and ended up sleeping together. I hated that narrative—the uncontrollable gay desire—why couldn't they have said something to me first? Derek didn't even tell me for a week.

But then I actually kind of liked seeing them together, except when they were arguing, and they were arguing right away. Whenever they got in a fight they both would call me, separately, and somehow it didn't feel uncomfortable to help them get along. It meant they needed me, we needed one another.

This was when everyone was talking about how expensive San Francisco was getting, but I found a cheap place in a huge flat in the Lower Haight with all these random people who talked endlessly about what they were doing for Burning Man—it was eight months away but they were already planning. One day, the person who had the lease came home from work with a vintage black Mercedes, and I knew something was strange. He had some kind of computer job, but people didn't use the word dot-com yet. At least not people I knew.

When I did go to the Mission, I looked at the buildings and all I could think about was death. Derek and I were planning to get an apartment together, but then he and Zee ended up moving to Oregon to work at a retreat center—I stood there at the bus station with tears in my eyes. I felt like they were leaving me. I mean they were leaving me.

Chrissie Contagious came to stay with me—remember

her, she was screaming naked in a tree when I met JoAnne. And Zee that same weekend, I guess that was only three years before but it already felt like decades. Chrissie was another of JoAnne's close friends—when someone so important to you dies like that you become closer to the others who are left: you have to.

This was when I decided that K was the only drug that was safe for me, it was the answer, and I ended up buying a ton of it for someone who then disappeared, so I figured I'd sell it, Chrissie and I could sell it together since she was the party girl. Although then I'd come home and she'd be cutting it up on my mirror. Oh well—might as well do some.

One night we went out to the Hole in the Wall, the bar that was the most popular for faggots trying to act like they weren't trendy, just masculine, they liked rock and beer and tattoos—if I wasn't having sex in the back then I was scaring everyone with runway. That night Chrissie met someone and afterwards they wanted to go to Blow Buddies. I'd never been to Blow Buddies—I'd heard it was just muscle queens, but I was never ready for bed when the bars closed. While we were in line, Chrissie's new fling took out a credit card and poured some crystal on it, then held it up to my nose. I'd always said people should do their drugs in public, so I got caught up in the moment and inhaled—everything shot to my head and I thought: Oh no, I've just ruined my life. And then: Might as well have fun.

So I ended up doing more crystal than ever before, but first we got kicked out of Blow Buddies for saying girl too much, and then Chrissie and the fling tried to fuck in my bed while I rearranged the room and tried to pretend I wasn't thinking about more crystal. Until they took it out again—oh, sure, just a little. Then Chrissie went to film a porn video and I was waiting at the End Up so I bought two more quarters, I was alternating it with huge bumps of K and on the dance floor it was like I was ten feet in the air but somehow my feet still touched the ground and I could bounce with the stars except it was daylight and I was still bouncing.

Maybe twenty hours of drugs later we were back at the Hole in the Wall. I figured I would do this huge bump of K, a whole capful, the kind of thing that normally would guarantee you a disastrous K-hole but I figured I'd be fine because all the crystal would keep me from getting catatonic. Soon enough I was sinking into the corner, the lights a toy for my eyes. I couldn't speak but I knew this feeling, I could play in my head. Until the bar started to close and since K wasn't big in San Francisco yet, they didn't know what it meant when my friends said oh, she's in a K-hole.

When I didn't move, the staff picked me up, carried me outside and dropped me onto the sidewalk. Then I couldn't get up off the ground because my head felt like it was cracking open there was so much pain. I was holding Rick's hand—I felt like if he let go I would be gone. I didn't mention Rick before but he was the one with barrettes who I told to leave Brown, and then he did, and when I got back to San Francisco he was there and turning tricks too and we would go to bars or try not to go to bars together, this time we ran into each other by coincidence and I was holding his hand because I could feel my life slipping away, eyes closed but everything was flying by. No one knew what to do until this homeless guy came over and said pour cold water on him and it'll bring him down, my friends weren't convinced but I nodded and they poured cold water on me and it worked.

After I recovered, which took a while, I mean if I ever recovered, I decided to stop drinking and go on a food elimination diet to figure out all my allergies—pretty much every time

I ate I felt sick, no matter how careful I tried to be. I figured I'd also go on the strictest anti-candida diet because when else wouldn't I be drinking? I wasn't drinking because alcohol just made me do drugs, the wrong drugs, maybe all drugs were the wrong drugs. I went to look for an apartment, but they all emphasized the credit check—my credit wasn't good and I didn't want to live in San Francisco anyway. I decided to move to Seattle so I could feel calm again.

WHAT WE WERE CREATING

W hen I moved back to San Francisco at the end of
2000, I went to a Chanukkah party. By this point
I generally didn't go to parties, even though I keep
writing about them, but a Chanukkah party sounded innocu-
ous enough. It was at the house of one of JoAnne's former
lovers, who lived less than a block from where we used to live.
It was the place where I stayed when I came back to San Francisco after JoAnne died, in Elyse's room—that room kind of
looked like the middle room in our old apartment, with one
window facing an air shaft, so when I first started writing this
I kept confusing that room with the one in our old place: Did
Elyse really move back in there? That didn't make sense. No, it
was down the street, and Andy was staying there too back then,
but I forgot about that until he mentioned it.

At that Chanukkah party five years later, I thought we
would be sitting around a table spinning dreidels and eating

latkes, but when I arrived the place was packed and the rooms were dim. Everyone was working the rocker junkie look—trucker caps and eyeliner, fake fur coats so ratty it looked like real animal skin was showing through. It was like the worst New York high-fashion disaster, except cheaper clothes and harder drugs. So many glazed eyes it was hard to keep track—heroin here, crystal there, acid in the hallway and there's the doorbell—cocaine!

This was the new San Francisco: peer around any corner in the Mission or South of Market and you'd see enormous luxury lofts that looked like they were made of particle board and aluminum. Drunk yuppies crowded the sidewalks in front of posh bars in the neighborhoods they used to make jokes about, while Hummers sped down side streets in search of parking. One famously cited driver admitted he ran over someone's grandmother to avoid spilling his cappuccino, inspiring a bus shelter ad campaign encouraging pedestrians and drivers to watch out for one another.

My friends had warned me about how awful San Francisco had become but they had also convinced me to move back, after a year in Seattle and three years in New York—we're you're family, they said. The two people who'd said that the most left the Bay Area within a few months of my return. Most people I knew had moved to Oakland and they said I should too—but Oakland wasn't like Brooklyn, you couldn't get around after midnight.

I needed to live in New York without New York: I knew that meant the Tenderloin. The dot-com frenzy was in full swing, so I found myself entering buildings without front doors, walking down bare hallways lit by exposed bulbs, to enter moldy $1200-a-month studio apartments facing out onto other people's fire escapes. Often I didn't even have enough time to wonder if it was possible to live in these dumps, because they were already taken. Or there would be a dozen people with computer jobs, checkbooks in hand, all vying for the manager or realtor's attention: Is the neighborhood safe? Is there anything nearby? How far is Union Square?

On my rental application, I became a technical writer who made a preposterous amount of money—everything except my name and social security number was fake. I got lucky, and ended up with a studio apartment on the top floor, set back from the street because of a burned-down building next door, facing Polk Street and the sun. Or, okay, maybe I didn't get that lucky—I had to outbid someone to get the lease, but it was the nicest and cheapest place I'd seen. I didn't know about the roaches or the rats or the pigeons yet, but the kitchen was big enough that I could put my bed in the dining area with a screen between sleep and vegetables, which felt luxurious. Certain people thought it was a strange set-up—why did they put the bedroom over there?

Of course, my technical writing consisted of giving blow jobs in plush, off-white hotel beds while the TV flashed stock prices behind me. I remember one Tuesday night, after my third trick and on my way to a fourth, stepping into the W and finding so many people in the lobby that they spilled into the elevators to make deals on their cell phones, cocktails in hand. Outside the Ritz-Carlton, there was a couple who looked like they couldn't be older than twenty-five, stepping out of a Rolls. The guy was wearing a waistcoat and holding a cigar in one hand and an attaché in the other, the woman was wearing a full-length fur and gold slip-on heels. At least I was making cash. In fact, I was making more than the figure on my rental application. After all, I had become a New York City hooker—no longer would I take the bus to save money, or turn down tricks who called when I was hanging out with a friend—I would show up within a half-hour, in full preppy drag. The tricks loved it. Sometimes they even asked if I was gay.

Back to the Mission, where it was no longer cool to be a dyke: you could be trans, or you could call yourself queer and refuse other labels. At this point, the trans guys who inhabited stereotypical masculine traits were the ones considered the hottest. The Eagle had become the trendiest bar for this particular scene, and no one talked about the long history of hostility at this and other leather bars toward women, people of color, and anyone perceived as feminine—now it was queer ground zero, the best place to go to hear bands. Certain faggots whispered cautiously about whether misogyny was a required part of transitioning into masculine realness. The most daring femmes joked about testosterone: Um, did somebody have too much T in their coffee? It seemed like there were a lot of trans guys rejecting everything they and I had learned in dyke cultures, not just the guys who wanted to pass or the ones who now identified as straight, but also those assimilating into gay culture—I mean, what could be worse than gay culture?

Later, trans guys would start doing drag in dresses, wearing pink, identifying as fags and not just in a denim-and-leather kind of way. Some would say: Fuck that tired excuse that testosterone makes us act like macho assholes, that's just biological essentialism. And ask: How can we remain accountable while assimilating into male privilege? And this would challenge my own assumptions about masculinity as something to be avoided: What would it mean to create a masculinity that was chosen, negotiated, and transformed?

Throughout all this, there was my relationship with Derek, the only friend left who I called family. He was getting more manic and more depressed, so nihilistic that sometimes it scared me—he would talk about buying a gun, he wanted to keep it under the bed. It didn't help when I told him I thought his medication was making everything worse, because I'd already expressed my disapproval beforehand. He kept changing meds and they were all horrible. When he started eating meat again, he said it was for health reasons, but then he would grab a hamburger at Burger King.

Derek was angry at me for judging him, but the hardest part was that he would lie about everything. He would go on some drinking binge and then tell me half of what happened, or half of the half he remembered, or wanted to remember, and I had to figure out what to believe. Sometimes it was obvious, like when he stopped to get cigarettes and came out of the store with a fifth of liquor in a paper bag—I thought you weren't drinking tonight, I said carefully. He'd already agreed that he wouldn't drink when we went out together, after I told him I couldn't deal with the way the friend who meant so much to me would become a macho asshole. When I asked him about the bottle in his hand, his face got all red with anger: I'm not drinking, this is a Coke. He might have even said: Why don't you trust me?

People were starting to talk about the dot-com crash but no one could tell the difference yet, I mean no one we knew. Derek and I heard about a squat party on Market Street. That sounded ridiculous—who were they kidding? It wouldn't last more than ten minutes. We headed over to see. We got to the address and it was a huge boarded-up theater, dozens of bikes locked up outside. We walked up the stairs into a cavernous room full of brightly painted murals and hundreds of people dancing to live music. Everyone was dressed to the nines in thrift-store artistry—sure, it was sceney as hell, but at least these were the kinds of weirdos I remembered. The party lasted for hours without interruption, and without the arrival of the cops. I wondered what else might be possible.

It's funny when your friends tell you you'll like someone, and then you meet that person and you're really not sure, but you decide to go with the recommendation anyway. So I went with Brodie to a party in Hayes Valley, a neighborhood almost completely colonized by fashion boutiques and interior design stores—I know what you're thinking: another party? Yes, let me tell you about another party.

This was a different scene—bourgie art fags trading barbs and trying to act scandalous. Or scandalized, depending on who was listening. The '70s gay clone look was very popular, and Brodie blended right in with his vintage denim. Of course this reminded me of New York—I thought of New York any-time I went someplace horrible.

There was '70s porn projected on the walls, which would have been fun in a sex space but here there were just fags in designer clothes talking about how dirty they were, but not as dirty as pussy. Brodie acted surprised when I went off on gay misogyny, not surprised that I was going off but surprised when I said it was consumed and assumed in pretty much ev-ery gay space. I wondered if, in his hope for belonging as a trans guy, Brodie was neglecting the obvious. Then he asked me what I was doing for Pride. Pride—was he kidding? Hiding inside my apartment—what else was there to do?

Returning to San Francisco and expecting to connect with a culture of radical queers that I imagined and remembered from the past, I was verging on hopelessness when faced with the reality of the present: if those cultures had ever existed in the ways I remembered, they did not exist in those ways now. Yes, there were plenty of edge-trendy scenesters looking for the coolest parties, but that was about it.

I started to tell Brodie about Gay Shame, and for once I got excited while talking about New York, where even though there were were far fewer radical-identified queers, we'd managed to create an alternative to Pride, and to make it into an annual event for a few years at Dumba. I fantasized aloud about taking Gay Shame further, bringing it to an outdoor space, something more public.

Brodie got excited too—let's do it, he urged. He was drunk. We only had a few weeks until Pride weekend—we would have to scout the location, make flyers, wheatpaste all over town, find performers and speakers and a sound system and DJs and who knew what else. That sounds so great, Brodie said. I was skeptical, but his enthusiasm turned on my manic button and then we were a team. We called everyone we knew, and started planning.

Several hundred people showed up to that first action at Tire Beach, a rotting industrial park on the San Francisco Bay where discarded streetcars ended up, and a concrete factory bordered a small area of grass and debris. The event was wild and festive, but people didn't seem that interested in the politics — they focused on drinking 40s out of paper bags, cheering for the bands but ignoring the speakers. Afterwards, we knew we were going to do it again, and many of us started brainstorming about how to connect the politics with the spectacle in a way that couldn't be separated.

Eventually we decided to directly confront the Pride parade the following year, but we figured we needed to create an action first to get people motivated, and that's when we came up with the Gay Shame Awards. We dressed to ragged excess and blocked the main intersection in the Castro with sofas, and then we held an awards ceremony, culminating with the burning of rainbow flags to recognize the most hypocritical gays for their service to the community in categories like Helping Right-Wingers Cope, Making More Queers Homeless, and Best Racist-Ass Whites-Only Space. We had stilt-walkers dressed in garbage bags, people handing out vegan food on silver trays; someone showed up in a dress made from shopping bags. Afterwards we held a dance party in the street, and queer youth of color who usually came to the Castro and found nothing to do joined in—even straight tourists were eagerly reading our official program.

We hadn't talked about making Gay Shame into a direct action activist group, but after the Awards it seemed like the momentum was there. Our weekly meetings continued, and sometimes several dozen people showed up. From the beginning, Gay Shame was a conscious attempt to bring the politics back into the party, but many of us disagreed about exactly what that meant: I wanted to make the politics into the party, and Brodie wanted to make the party into the politics. Maybe that sounds like the same thing, but actually this tension stretches back through decades of queer organizing. Perhaps one difference from generations before was that neither of us talked about the politics versus the party, but still it felt that way when we argued about the direction we wanted Gay Shame to take, argued inside and outside meetings where battle lines were drawn, relationships made and unmade.

We talked about Gay Shame as an amorphous and ever-changing we, but the truth is that initially the rhetoric came from me, and it was Brodie, with his years in the Mission scene, who brought the numbers. I was the MC for every protest, delivering a scathing incantation in lavish outfits made of glitter and tattered gowns. Brodie's talents lay more in the mechanics and mobilization of each event. And although Gay Shame always made decisions by consensus, for the first big actions it was the two of us who made sure everything came together—if either of us had stopped our manic involvement, Gay Shame probably would have ended.

If activists demand leaders even when engaging in non-hierarchical work, the media requires them: I was the one who created the sound bites, and in the public eye I became Gay Shame; and perhaps this made sense because when I said we wanted to create a home for the culturally homeless, I also meant that I didn't want to give up. When I said we wanted to build our own culture on the ruins of the rot surrounding us, I also meant that Gay Shame gave me hope in radical queer dreams, in creating community through critique, relationships through activism, accountability through action. I needed that hope.

I met Ralowe at that first Gay Shame action at Tire Beach, a queer autonomous space in the industrial ruins of our lives. I'm not sure exactly what made me think he was a well-meaning straight guy at first, something about how he carried masculinity and it carried him; I'm sure Ralowe will hate that description. Later we would talk about his difficulties as a black fag existing in mostly white countercultures, and he would wonder if that's what made me think he was straight the first time we met, and even the second time, when he talked about going to the Power Exchange. Until he started talking about sucking cock at the glory holes there, and even then it was in this strange pornographic way that made it seem like he was talking about someone else talking about someone like him.

Ralowe started coming to meetings right away, once Gay Shame held regular meetings—he always had the most outrageous ideas. Like when we were planning our confrontation with the Pride parade, and he suggested we hook up a hose to raw sewage and spray it on the crowd. Sometimes he would start rapping in the middle of a meeting, or yelling at someone because he thought they said something stupid.

But then Ralowe would come up with something that sounded nonsensical, like rainbow Klan outfits, and everyone would wonder: What the hell are you talking about? It was like she was trying to provoke the group into doing something that would be perceived as racist, in order to challenge the racism of the gay mainstream. But then she kept repeating: the evil Gay Gay Gay, rainbow Klan outfits, the evil Gay Gay Gay, rainbow Klan outfits—her eyes would glaze over, but it actually started to make sense to me. I'm switching pronouns here, because I do that all the time, but also because here is where Ralowe decided to reject the male pronoun in favor of the queen's worldview, even if, and maybe especially because, all her contradictions remained.

Ralowe's ideas often seemed ridiculous, but I sensed something exciting that I wanted to make clear, even if Ralowe talked about not wanting to see things in a rational way. I was looking for allies, and we began to process the meetings together after the others had left. We both wanted the group to focus on direct action, not spend energy organizing cool parties for the Mission scene.

I wasn't interested in Gay Shame as a social identity outside of activism—at bars and parties and wherever else—even though my relationships were facilitated through Gay Shame actions, since that's how I ended up meeting all my closest friends. And really, I was in a privileged position because of my role in starting Gay Shame: I didn't need to go to the parties in order to get people to pay attention to me.

So there I was, hating the Mission scene and helping to create it—our meetings always took place in the Mission; most of the people who showed up at our demos lived or socialized in the Mission. But here's the thing: people would come to our meetings, and it would change them. Ralowe was one of those people—she'd never been involved in direct action before, and suddenly she became so enthusiastic that sometimes it felt oppressive. In meetings when she would make some over-the-top declaration, most people would stare in that blank way that meant someone just said something crazy. I'm not suggesting that I didn't think she was crazy, but I believed in crazy—we were all crazy, wasn't that the point?

But here's what Socket has to say: I think the social and the political parts of Gay Shame were more merged—you're drawing a really clear distinction but most people didn't see it that way. You were a social commodity, and when you were really popular the group was really popular—you were the central character and people moved around you. A lot of it was just mirroring. I was reading about Huey Newton at the time, and the cult of personality, and I wondered if this was it. To be honest, I came because of you, that's why I was there. When you recruited me to teach people how to do police negotiation, I remember saying to take down badge numbers, or to repeat the officers' names over and over, for subversive intimidation, and people thought I had created that idea—they didn't have organizing experience. They listened to me because I was your friend. They were cute and sweet and interesting, partiers and drinkers and artists and creative types, but not organizers or activists. Gay Shame brought the intellectual and non-intellectual together, it was the opposite of boring. Remember that action with the Vomitorium?

Me: Of course—when we were confronting the Pride parade, and we made that big Budweiser can out of cardboard and you could go inside and vomit out your Budweiser pride.

And we also brought official Gay Shame vomit bags, in case you couldn't make it to the Vomitorium in time.

Socket: That was brilliant and raunchy and so much more enticing than the organizing I was used to. It was that merging of the social and political that made Gay Shame so sexy. And people were willing to take political risks. But most people left during all the processing, they weren't interested in doing that kind of work. And around then I was talking to someone about Gay Shame, and they said oh, you mean Mattilda's children?

Me: But who did they mean?

Socket: They meant everyone, even though there were people older than you and you didn't want to be that kind of leader. But at the same time you were. You had a strong hand on the framing of everything and how things were worded, the performance, the slogans, it was a social enclave you had created. And you were so dedicated to this process of open meetings, consensus, so when my friend said "Mattilda's children" of course it was meant to be shady, and when I didn't mention it to you I felt kind of complicit. Because I wanted you to know what people were saying, except I couldn't think of a way to acknowledge that it was fucked up, but that there was still a critique worth hearing.

Me: I knew people were saying all kinds of things, but I didn't want that to get in the way of our organizing. When someone would try to tell me something like that, I would say I don't want to hear that stupid shit.

Socket: I think that's what you said to me. But you were really in this role where you were teaching people something totally new.

Me: But that's not how I thought about it, I didn't want that kind of power. I thought we were meeting each other on our own terms. It took me a while to realize that sometimes people would just say what I wanted to hear, that it gave them credibility to be friends with me, that I was this sort of status object. But I don't think that happened as much at meetings.

Socket: You thought people had the political analysis, but they didn't, the social and political were all combined, they were never very distinct. So all the partying, even though you weren't doing it, it became a Gay Shame thing, and since you weren't doing it you didn't have the same influence over how it happened, or how people treated one another, that you did in meetings or at actions. I remember going to parties where people would get really messy and sexually desperate and treat each other like shit.

Me: That's why I didn't go to those parties, because then I would see how people acted, and I wouldn't want to do activism with them. And I didn't want to sleep with people in the group because of the way it would play out at meetings.

Socket: So for you it was about transparency, and that's why you're drawing a distinction between what happened at meetings and what happened outside, because what happened at meetings was transparent, it was a shared value. But if half of the people weren't transparent about anything else in the rest of their lives, then I don't think they were really getting it.

Me: For me the important thing was what we were creating together. I do remember I wanted to start an affinity group with you and a few of the other people who I really trusted, like Derek.

Socket: But I never trusted Derek.

Me: I know.

But you remember the Eagle, right? At some point the manager approached Brodie and asked if we wanted to do a benefit there. The idea of a benefit at a white gay male space entrenched in traditional gay bar norms of mandatory masculinity, routine misogyny, and racial exclusion split the group—those who loved the Eagle loved the idea, but the rest of us were skeptical. If we held a benefit there, wouldn't we be tacitly accepting their policies? Or worse, would we be giving them cover? I mean, the fact that the bar had become a hot spot for the Mission scene on Thursdays didn't mean that anything else had really changed.

The Eagle benefit was financially successful, but it brought group tensions to the surface. Many of us were appalled to find ourselves surrounded by the apolitical scenesters who never came to our demos, swarming around us in a sea of beer. But we did get excited when someone noticed a newspaper ad promoting an event for Gavin Newsom, at this point a wealthy city council member whose claim to fame was Care Not Cash, a ballot measure that took away homeless peoples' welfare benefits and replaced them with "care." Now that he had successfully built a career by criminalizing the most vulnerable in San Francisco, he was pandering to gay power brokers by holding a fundraising benefit for the LGBT Center to be held in one week. And get this: Newsom's Valentine's benefit was called "Hot Pink"—what an opportunity for outfits.

We decided on the spot that we had to be there, but when I started to announce the upcoming festivity, Eagle staff turned off the microphone, telling me I was too loud, my queeny voice too irritating. Louder and more irritating, apparently, than the three bands performing that evening. I told the bartender we weren't just there to make money for the Eagle, we actually wanted to promote our actions. He told me: You need to stop prancing around in here.

I was enraged—I went over to Brodie and told him the story, but he just stared at me with a drunk, glazed look in his eyes. I guess we were still friends afterwards, but I didn't believe in him anymore. Later that night, after a femme friend in a band confronted the manager, he approached me to explain that the Eagle didn't allow people to announce outside events. When I told him that was ridiculous, he pushed me halfway across the bar, then picked me up and forced me out the door.

Worse than this incident was the unwillingness of many Gay Shame organizers to critique the Eagle—they're part of our community, people whined. Since we had formed Gay Shame specifically to expose the violence that lurks beneath this type of rhetoric, it was particularly unnerving to hear it at our meetings.

Maybe it sounds strange that queer women and trans guys were the ones seeking to shield a gay male leather bar from critique, but this was that same loyalty I had witnessed in the early '90s—loyalty to social status and scene over critical engagement. In the queer Mission scene, dykes and trans guys in bands and bars inhabited the center—they were the ones who threw the parties and knew how to party, or at least knew where the party was. Everyone else remained on the sidelines: most fags and anyone who was unwilling or unable to play by the rules of hipster disengagement.

This was one of the battle lines at Gay Shame meetings: Were we there to create a space for the people who didn't fit in? I'm sure everyone would have answered yes, but they would've meant entirely different things. Later, once Gay Shame lost its trendiness, we became a smaller, more alienated group consisting mostly of fags. We might have looked more uniform from the outside, but we felt persecuted by the lack of options for radical queer visions in the spaces that were supposedly radical and queer.

A week after the Eagle incident we went to the Center to confront Newsom. The cops were already there to block us from entering. Newsom arrived and a phalanx of cops escorted him through the glass doors. I was thrown by a police baton into oncoming traffic, and probably would have tumbled face-first onto the asphalt if it wasn't for Zee, who broke my fall, and we fell together into the middle of the street. Four of us were arrested. One arrestee was put into a choke hold until she passed out. Afterwards, a cop hit one protester in the face with his club: a photo capturing blood dripping down that person's face ended up in local papers.

That night was emotional for other reasons too: Zee and I were no longer close, but there he was catching my fall. Crying inside the police van, of course we couldn't help but remember how we'd met and bonded inside a different police van, although that time we'd planned in advance for our arrests. This time I was worried about the pain in my wrists—my fingers were turning blue, and I asked an officer to loosen my cuffs. He tightened them. I was released first, in part because my hands were so swollen that even jail staff looked worried.

This feels like it's becoming a history of Gay Shame, but that's not what I'm trying to write. What I want is to map the relationships I formed through our actions, to illuminate the contradictions that I can see more clearly now. Maybe then I won't feel so lost.

But here we are, almost two years into this, and Eric hasn't even made an appearance. I mean, she's the one who showed up at our demos with handmade Gay Shame buttons featuring pictures of Rosie O'Donnell and George Michael, actualizing the dream of participation we were invoking, but she lived and went to school in Santa Cruz so it took a while before she started coming to meetings.

We first bonded at an academic conference calling itself "Gay Shame," an illustrious queer theory shindig in Michigan that invited our participation on one panel—the organizers became enraged when we proposed a critique of their appropriation. A famous attendee yelled that I was "just like Cheney," implying that by critiquing the academy we were furthering the goals of the Christian right. Later that night, Eric and I commiserated out of that strange combination of alienation and kinship that always feels so hopeful to me. We talked for hours, two nights in a row, sharing life stories that looped around one another in an embrace. Eric was as critical as I was. He was on the way to becoming the first person in his family to graduate from college, but he wasn't buying into the myths of upward mobility. He'd dropped out of high school to run away from his parents at age fourteen and he'd spent years in outsider queer cultures, so he recognized the hypocrisy of institutionalized violence masquerading as critical engagement.

We talked about growing up and abuse and escaping and veganism and cooking and drugs. I remember talking about Boston and one devastating K-hole or another—if I was talking about growing up and abuse and escaping then I had to talk about at least one K-hole. Eric said he'd never done drugs—it always confused me when I met someone who hadn't done drugs, especially another fag, but Eric said he'd seen the way heroin surrounded his friends and he already felt surrounded enough. We talked about sex, so of course I talked about sex work and how it was starting to feel like a trap. No, it had felt like a trap for a long time—maybe it was kind of like academia was for Eric, a certain kind of safety through something we were never supposed to know. We talked about relationships and romance and what we were looking for, Eric was in a monogamous relationship. I asked what that meant for him. He said it was the only way he felt safe—he didn't feel like it was better or worse politically or ethically, it was just what worked for him.

I know I have a certain model for relationships, based in those first conversations about incest and accountability, sexual striving and loss, hopelessness and rage and other unwavering queer dreams. A model that says: First you reveal everything, and then when you can't think of anything else to reveal you go deeper. And: It's us against the world. That relationship model was one of the reasons I came back to San Francisco, but then the relationships weren't there. It's possible that even the model had burned down in some landlord-induced fire in the Mission, insurance money and new condos.

In a way, my friendship with Eric felt the closest to this ideal, and it reminded me of the beginnings of my foundational relationships, where we connected by sharing our complicated histories, an act of intimacy through disclosure. But maybe those late-night conversations where we came together over the shock of immediate threats to our shared visions made us feel closer than we actually were.

I felt frustrated by my relationships: they would get to a certain point of political or intellectual intimacy, emotional too, but then I always wanted to get to the next level—I wanted an embodied feeling of closeness. I recognized the push-pull of intimacy, but when I felt the other person was doing most of the pulling away, eventually I would give up. I wouldn't give up on the relationship, but I would give up thinking it would go further. I was already retreating more into my head, as chronic pain and exhaustion overwhelmed the everyday and I started worrying that soon I would be the one who wouldn't be able to move into a deeper intimacy.

Still there was Derek, emerging from his alcoholism but not from a secrecy that meant the safety I treasured often felt elusive. I'd learned that critique wasn't necessarily love, but with Derek I'd become overly cautious—I'd spend months thinking about something he'd lied about, trying to think of a way to bring it up without making him feel threatened. I thought I was avoiding the drama, but really it was all just staying inside me. Maybe that was one of the reasons I was always so exhausted.

My sleep felt worthless: I would stay in bed as long as possible, sometimes more than twelve hours to try to experience any kind of rest, but I always woke up feeling worse. I would stumble out of bed, my whole body aching, my jaw so tense it felt like there were bruises all over my face, my arms burning from what the specialists first called repetitive stress injury, then tendinitis, now fibromyalgia. But where was this horrible headache coming from, like a drill burrowing into the space between my eyebrows and then surrounding me on all sides. I had to cook, so I would start chopping vegetables even though using the knife gave me shooting pains in my arms, and then I would sit at the computer trying in vain to get the voice activation software to type even a sentence that would make sense.

Ralowe acknowledged this place of crisis in my body— she wanted to help, it felt crucial to her. She would come over to my house once a week, and we would get groceries, do laundry, go to the post office; she would chop vegetables and type for me. I would buy groceries for her, pay for memory cards for her music, buy dinner or offer to pay for other things that she needed, so there was a financial dimension, but it wasn't defined as a response to her assistance. I offered to pay her directly, but she didn't want our relationship to be monetized: I respected that.

Really what I gave most in return was attention. Every week, Ralowe and I would spend hours talking through the crises that emerged in her life. Sometimes it was about the queen in her building who gave her class shade, even though or especially because they were both black fags living in subsidized housing. Or the fictitious white profile Ralowe created on chat sites to cruise the guys who would never pay attention to her. We talked about whether it was possible for her to perform music in public without becoming another fetish object for white scenesters, the undercover cops outside her window, the way white people fidgeted on the street like she was going to attack them, the way black people on the bus talked about her like she was trash, whether video games were the key to unlocking mass consciousness, the posturing of indie white rappers, the relentlessness of gentrification in the Mission, and what it had been like growing up in a white suburb in Southern California.

Ralowe's stories would zoom into past and future at once, and sometimes both were dead ends, like the white childhood friend who tried to kiss her, but she pushed him away and now she was trying to track him down on a military base and maybe they would become lovers. But Ralowe was also trying to envision practical solutions to everyday trauma, and we talked about her ex-boyfriend, racialized desire, objectification, consumerism, pubic lice, SSI, and whether it was possible to cook your own food and get out of the house too.

We were both obsessed in our own ways with music and graffiti and public space and trying to figure out a sexuality that didn't just feel like loss, but mostly we connected out of a shared alienation we had learned to politicize. Or a shared alienation that I had learned to politicize, that Ralowe was learning. She would often become judgmental in the way that usually happens at points of activist emergence, as if there was only one true path to radical engagement. I remember when I thought anyone who wasn't vegan was a disaster, right? Or, when I thought I was a horrible person because I'd eaten a piece of chewing gum that might have contained sugar processed with animal bones.

I would talk with Ralowe about everything in my life too, but in a different way—I rarely asked for help beyond the physical tasks that overwhelmed me. Sometimes it was fun to brainstorm a particularly wacky word choice, but when I did ask for emotional support, I wasn't even sure that Ralowe noticed—on the phone, I would hear the keyboard clicking in the background. How could she listen to me if she was on MySpace or cruising Gay.com? But her help in the daily tasks of my life felt so generous that it overrode my reservations about other aspects of our friendship. I thought that maybe it balanced itself out when she would help me chop vegetables, and in return I would help her think things through. Not that either of us planned our relationship this way, but it's how it developed.

Sometimes on those Mondays we spent together I would get frantic too because there was so much I wanted to get done, but still I was trying to appear outwardly calm, to make sure Ralowe knew I felt grateful. Actually we spent every Saturday together too, after the Gay Shame meeting, and then often another few times for smaller group meetings, wheatpasting, or stenciling. Our friendship became a primary relationship—we weren't just committed to a queer politic of challenging the violence of the status quo and creating alternatives, we were committed to one another.

I wanted this to feel like home, hope, an embrace, safety, but sometimes it seemed like the only way Ralowe could experience comfort was to make everyone else uncomfortable. Even walking down the street together was stressful for her, she would glimpse the limitations of other people's interpretations and this would make her deranged. She noticed that people smiled at me, and this enraged her. She was worried that alongside my white queeniness her masculinity became emphasized. Or that people might perceive her as just another black man helping some white person. She would dress more flamboyantly, trying to invoke my queeniness in order to see if people would react to her like they did to me. But this didn't change her masculine demeanor—people looked at her like she was confused.

Of course, people looked at me like I was confused too. But I'd spent years developing a kind of ease that made it appear like anything could happen and I would just walk on. While Ralowe avoided looking at anyone directly, I greeted people on the street as if I knew them—I reacted to shady comments as if they were applause. It was hard for Ralowe to ignore people's reactions, but it was harder for her to be ignored, and often that's what happened when we went out together—I think this disturbed her as much as anything else. She would get all frantic and start yelling like some imagined frat boy in a porn video. She needed whatever attention would come her way, even if she had to act like a misogynist sex-crazed zombie to get it: the seamlessness I was trying to enact made her more desperate.

Really I was so exhausted that it was hard for me to walk the six blocks to get groceries—usually I had to stop and sit down on the way, or eat a snack when I got hypoglycemic. I needed a break, but when I started to say something Ralowe's eyes would glaze over and she would rap at me, an onslaught of someone else's lyrics at full volume, and I wondered if she was trading one embodied aggression for another, and why it was directed at me.

I watched the ways people related to Ralowe at Gay Shame meetings, when she would start screaming about the new Tarantino movie, some blockbuster video game, or the current rapper she was obsessed with, or when she would yell at a new person in the room for some unintelligible reason, scaring that person away for good. Or when we would go wheatpasting and Ralowe would volunteer as lookout, but instead of keeping a discreet distance and watching for cops she would start jumping up in the air and screaming at the top of her lungs.

Ralowe's behavior didn't faze Eric—she would just nod her head and move on. It was harder for me because Ralowe and I spent so much time together, but also because I wanted our relationship to become deeper, softer, more nurturing. I wanted to stay emotionally engaged, but often this meant the dynamic between us felt parental to me: Ralowe would say something completely ridiculous to provoke me and I would try to stay calm but eventually crack. We were basically the same age, but direct action, veganism, queeniness, sex work, and an outsider queer identity were all new to Ralowe. Maybe it was inevitable that there would be some kind of power differential—but I had lived my whole life avoiding parental figures, and I wasn't interested in becoming one: even mentorship seemed suspicious to me.

It's true that some of the best Gay Shame propaganda existed in that tension between my calculated satire and Ralowe's swinging off the earth—when it worked there was a wicked glee in the resulting flyers, press releases, and posters usually forged in small group meetings in my apartment. But if the process was as important as the product, the dynamic that emerged between the two of us could hardly have invited participation from anyone who couldn't interrupt.

When Ralowe suddenly started wearing bright colors and vintage thrift-store styles I thought well, maybe she's just getting more flamboyant. Like with gender: I could sense that I'd inspired her to embrace the queen's vernacular, but then she did her fair share of wacky things like twisting he and she around so much that really you had no idea what she was talking about—that was her style. At one point Ralowe started wearing a French-cuff shirt with the cuffs undone, one of my trademarks, and one of the other black queens in the Mission said oh no, now there are two Mattildas. That's when I knew I wasn't just imagining it. When I said something, Ralowe told me I was copying her hair—my hair was big and spiky at the time, but it couldn't quite compare to her Afro.

Our relationship came apart when Ralowe told me she was worried I was compromising my integrity by deciding to visit my father as he was dying. I had taken the train cross-country, and was about to see my father in the house where I grew up with all his violence. Eleven years before, I'd told my father I would never speak to him again unless he acknowledged that he had sexually abused me. He hadn't acknowledged anything. My decision to visit him anyway challenged Ralowe's opinion of me, and somehow she thought the most supportive thing she could do was to question my integrity. Then she wanted to talk about the *Wall Street Journal*.

A few months earlier, a reporter from the *Wall Street Journal* had approached Gay Shame to do an interview. He had seen some of our wheatpastes about gentrification on Polk Street. Of course we were skeptical, but we made a consensus decision to go through with it—it's not like anyone else was going to be talking critically about gentrification in the *Wall Street Journal,* maybe we could at least get in a good quote or two. I volunteered to do the interview, since I was living on Polk Street myself and knew the most about it. I put together a modified business outfit complete with a frosted asymmetrical mullet and smeared lipstick, and gave a detailed description of the gentrification and its effects.

Now the predictably unsympathetic article had landed on the front page, and the reporter had used my legal name as attribution instead of Mary Hedgefunds, the name I'd given him. Ralowe told me she didn't trust my account of the interview, she thought I was trying to use the *Wall Street Journal* for my own advantage.

Ralowe didn't trust media at all, any media, not even the tiniest, most radical independent outlets. And yet she felt it was necessary, crucial even, to confront me about an interview with a publication owned by the stock exchange, just as I was about to visit my father on his deathbed. I felt like she was using the language of accountability without the substance, and I wondered if she actually knew what accountability meant.

I want to say that at some point Ralowe, Eric, and I started talking about the ways in which Gay Shame was becoming a conversation between the three of us. People would look to us for ideas, motivation, inspiration—we were the ones who held it together. But actually I'm not sure if the three of us ever talked about this dynamic directly. One on one, for sure, but never as a trio. I felt like Gay Shame was stuck—the only new people we attracted were college graduates who had just moved to San Francisco, and grad students who were studying us; they would get bored, or the semester would end. Everyone else had already decided Gay Shame didn't belong to them: we were too cool or not cool enough, too angry or jaded or crazy or intellectual or stupid or frivolous or serious, too slow or impulsive or cliquish or political or young or messy or artsy or ridiculous. Our alienation felt creative and our politics remained rigorous, but our activities became sporadic—we would come up with grand ideas, but without a critical mass it felt harder to take risks. And risks had always been our strong point.

I wondered if we should end Gay Shame with a grand

finale, and brainstorm new interventions. But I didn't want to suggest bringing the group to a close just because it had ceased to inspire me; I asked Ralowe and Eric what they thought. I could tell they were frightened by my suggestion—the group as it currently existed had become more a part of their identities than mine. I remained dedicated because I believed in these friendships that had emerged through our activism together: maybe that was enough.

Before I went to visit my father, I told Ralowe that I wanted our relationship to grow deeper, more relaxed—her purposeful craziness felt like a cover for doing whatever she wanted, regardless of the impact on other people: I didn't like arguing with her all the time. Our conversation went in circles—every time it felt like we were getting somewhere, she would say: Actually, that's not what I meant. And then, a few weeks later, when she told me I was using the *Wall Street Journal* for my own advantage, she acted as if there was a crisis in Gay Shame, all these unnamed people who didn't trust me but they couldn't say anything: she was speaking for them, a noble act, because of our closeness.

I wanted every relationship to build toward the intimacy I felt with Derek, that soft shelter in our eyes—when we were together I could feel that place in my body where I knew safety. At least when I wasn't worried our relationship was going to fall apart.

The interview I gave with the *Wall Street Journal* was about the end of San Francisco as a place where marginalized queers could try to figure out a way to cope. I was talking about Polk Street, one of the last remaining public spaces for homeless youth, hustlers, trans women, street queens, drug addicts, seniors on disability, and migrants of all types, but fast becoming a hot destination for fashionistas and office drones to sip green apple martinis. The *Wall Street Journal* didn't exactly talk about this form of ethnic cleansing—they decided Gay Shame was fighting for the neighborhood's "gritty ambience." But the article did reveal that Larkin Street Youth Services hired out the kids in their shelter to plant palm trees in front of the architecture firm spearheading the gentrification, at the preposterous rate of six dollars a day. And it reprinted the WANTED poster we'd made for the head of that architecture firm.

My apartment overlooked Polk Street, and whenever I walked around I could see the neighborhood disappearing: the closure of the gay porn shop that had been open since the '60s; beat cops on the hustling block; the old gentlemen's bar transformed into a straight rocker-chic hot spot; two hustler bars renovated into sleek lounges; the last hustler bar torn down to make way for a church. But it was hard to figure out what Gay Shame could do—while some of us were hookers, some of us runaways, and some of us certainly did drugs, none of us was turning tricks on the street to get a room for the night, hustling for a shot of speed, or asking for spare change outside the liquor store. We all belonged, in some form or another, to a counterculture that meant we could politicize our dissent. If we held one of our typical protests, we were certain to draw our usual crowd of Mission scenesters decked out in ragged extravagance; we worried that the spectacle we would bring to the neighborhood wouldn't be that different from the gentrification we wanted to challenge. Or that's what I worried anyway. That's where I got stuck.

Ralowe and I had many conversations about the *Wall Street Journal*, about Gay Shame, and about our relationship. Some of these conversations went further than others. One of the best ones started when I said: I don't have any other relationships that are so incredibly giving, but also so uncomfortable—I want to feel confident that if I call you when I'm feeling stressed out, I'll feel better afterwards, not disconnected and hopeless. I want to be able to hang out with you for a day and not feel completely drained afterwards.

Ralowe: I don't have that kind of relationship with anyone, I don't even want that.

Me: That's the problem, because you have what you want from our relationship, and I don't.

Ralowe: I need to know that there's space for my personality, that it's an accepted thing that I'm oblivious and I have a constant need to start shit.

Me: My only way to deal with that is to disengage, and I don't want to constantly disengage from someone I love, the person who I've spent the most time with over the last three years—we've both invested so much energy working on our relationship. I can't deal with you constantly attacking me all the time.

Ralowe: I feel like you're making an ultimatum. I get so frustrated with the things I say about how I'm feeling when what's really bothering me is something different that I can't even figure out how to talk about. I notice that I develop new ways to process going down the street every day because I forget the old ways, and maybe I need to be supported in that. Except that if I sensed support, then I wouldn't accept it or I wouldn't know what it was and I guess I feel better if I always think that no matter how sunny or beautiful a day, something awful is going to happen—otherwise I'll be shocked that someone's acting in a racist way, or that there's a cop on my corner. And I guess I need to project this frustration, and make you frustrated, so that I don't have to feel so alone.

Before I went to visit my father, before the *Wall Street Journal* interview, and before all these conversations, Ralowe spotted the signs announcing the new Museum of the African Diaspora—she wondered about white passersby clutching purses and briefcases tighter as they passed what could be double trouble: a black male with an Afro outside a construction site labeled African Diaspora. When the museum opened, Ralowe asked me if I wanted to go.

The Museum of the African Diaspora was a project of San Francisco's former mayor, Willie Brown, a black man who famously declared that if you couldn't afford to live in San Francisco, then you should just leave. After promoting the dot-com gentrification and helping to rid San Francisco of as many black people as possible, he decided to create a museum in their honor. In the lobby we saw the themes of the museum elaborated on the walls: Origins, Movement, Adaptation, Transformation. The place felt like a cross between a rec center, an airport lounge, and a preschool: gray carpet, indeterminate hues of green or blue paint on the walls, and exhibits that looked like something Bank of America would display in the lobby and you'd say oh, that's nice—can I check my balance?

Since Ralowe and I were the only visitors, we were outnumbered at least three-to-one by security guards. At one point an upscale Asian woman came out of an office to scold two members of the all-black security staff, since they had accidentally allowed Ralowe and me to enter the administrative section. One of the guards was so friendly, though, that she almost seemed like a docent. She told us where to start—it's a celebration circle, she said. We entered a circular room with a cheesy video describing all the important things in life: Family, Church, Births, Weddings, Death. At the end of the video we were treated to an inspiring message: We All Come from Africa.

On our way out, the friendly security guard asked if we liked the museum—I sensed that she felt a certain kind of pride, and I was too stunned not to tell her yes. I even smiled. Ralowe didn't respond. She showed me the hotel next door, the glittering St. Regis, where I'd read that rooms started at $529, and the penthouse condominium was rumored to be on the market for $30 million. The museum had been built into a back corner of the hotel, since that was part of the deal: You get fifty stories of luxury on city-owned land, as long as you allow us the space to open this charade. The hotel lobby looked like a posh nightclub, with startlingly high ceilings and huge beige curtains dividing lounge areas where big white men with swept-back hair, wearing suits with oversized shoulder pads, sipped cocktails on European leather sofas alongside tiny women with tasteful blond highlights and low-cut evening dresses.

Ralowe and I walked around the corner to the bus stop across the street from the entrance to Neiman Marcus. I couldn't stop thinking about that security guard asking me if I liked the museum, she sounded so excited. I found myself staring at the entrance to Neiman Marcus, thinking about all the ways to actively participate in white supremacy, and Ralowe asked if I was okay. I couldn't say anything—that's when I started crying, really crying—I was thinking about the audacity of Willie Brown for brokering another corporate give-away, then sheltering it with promotional materials that talked about this pioneering institution, the first of its kind in the world. Ralowe was sitting next to me, and I knew it was ironic that I was the one breaking down, but maybe this was our closest moment together.

UNLEARNING THE SAFETY

I've been thinking about this conversation for weeks, especially last week when we were supposed to talk but then Derek had three nights of particularly awful sleep and so he canceled. That made sense. But last week I was ready because I actually slept okay and I figured out the two things I needed to say. Now I'm not ready at all—I'm too worried: I'm afraid of losing the only relationship that makes me feel safe. I'm afraid of continuing our friendship but losing the possibility of that intimacy that goes on and on. I'm afraid of Derek.

I look at the red velvet pillow on the sofa and think: That's the pillow Derek leans against. I put sauerkraut on my plate, and think: That's the sauerkraut Derek made for me. I hear the lights humming, and think: That's because of the dimmer switch Derek installed.

At first we're talking about random things but neither of us seems interested and I'm just scared. So scared that even though I decided I was going to talk first, talk right away and say those two things, because usually I ask Derek how he's feeling first and that didn't work the last two times, even though I decided I would speak first, I can't speak.

Derek starts talking about how he still feels angry but his eyes are here, not far away like last time, still on me in a way that means I'm here, we're here, we're here together. He's telling me I was talking about things that were so old and he's changed, he's a different person. He can't deal with that kind of processing. He's telling me it doesn't serve him anymore to think about something obsessively from all angles so now he's trying to look at it from a distance. He's telling me it's hard for him when I talk for a long time without interruption, it's overwhelming, and maybe there's a different way we can talk.

Oh wait, he's asking me, he's asking me and I'm trying to say something. I close my eyes. I'm afraid to say that the last conversation was really scary for me.

Derek says do you think it's okay to have this conversation now?

Because I keep going to the bathroom to shit—I can't digest anything. I say no, it's fine, I'm just scared.

I look him in the eyes—this time he doesn't do that thing like he's in the military and we're in a staring contest so if I look away I'm dead, but I still can't say what I want to say. I start to speak but it's just a mumble, I'm looking into the distance then my eyes are closed then I'm looking up then my eyes are closed again and I feel like crying but I can't and I'm kind of shaking maybe there's a tear or two and I try to look at Derek. I say: I'm having trouble speaking.

My feet, pay attention to my feet is what I'm thinking. My feet on the ground, are my feet on the ground, my butt on this chair, my shoulders am I holding my shoulders back too far? I'm trying to avoid ending up in too much pain afterwards. I'm thinking about my list of two things, two things, what are those two things? I notice the list underneath a piece of paper Derek is studying, the directions for the shower filter.

I say: It was really hard for me last time. It was hard because you were speaking to me in such a dismissive way, with so much anger and disdain and I've never felt that before except with my father. It felt violent. I felt like you were requiring me to shut myself off emotionally like I did as a kid. It felt like you wanted me to shut off. I still haven't cried. I can't cry and I feel more distant, distant from everything.

It takes a while for me to say each sentence broken up into parts. And then: I know this wasn't going to happen, but I felt like you were going to hit me.

Now there's that smile on Derek's face like I just said something preposterous. Like I'm preposterous. I think okay, this is the end. But I say: That's the dismissiveness I'm talking about. And he stops.

I'm shaking, suddenly freezing. I go to the closet to put on a wool sweater, and then I'm in the bathroom again I should just keep shaking to let it out my hands all clammy I lean my head back oh it feels like I'm high keep me in the sky I mean really really high and I wonder about the difference between dissociation and staying present.

This is the second or maybe third no fourth time in the bathroom already, two times shitting and two times shaking, back in the kitchen I say I don't know why I'm so cold. Derek is telling me I talked for ten minutes without stopping I just kept going on and on it was hard for him to listen it made him so angry.

I get up and go into the living room to stretch because I'm

shaking too much, but then it's like I can't breathe I start to choke so I go back in the kitchen to gargle saltwater.

I sit back down and close my eyes. Breathe, breathe. Breathe.

The world suddenly feels like a different place and I'm scared I can't fit into it in the ways I want to, that I'll never again fit into it in those ways. In my body walking through streets and sitting on sofas and talking to friends and crying and laughing, I know I will do all these things but I wonder about getting back to that place of safety in my body.

I can tell Derek is getting emotional too, not just angry, and what I want is to hug him. I'm thinking yes, I can take that risk, yes, it's worth it. But I can't speak.

Finally I say: Do you want a hug? He says yes, and we stand, and he's the one who starts crying. I feel my body in a different way my body with him in the way I want it's a long hug I like this hug I don't want it to end. Except also I'm wondering if this is the future—I'm present for Derek, but is he present for me? I brush the hair above his ears with my fingers.

The hug is over so I sit down but Derek is still standing. He says: I feel like I'm doing all this work on myself, I've been doing all this work and it's finally working. I spend all this time with people in AA who are mostly concerned with buying this and buying that, but I can also feel things for these people and I used to get scared I would become someone like them or I would lose my sense of self. I know the world is still a horrible horrible place, but sometimes I feel like maybe I can be happy and last time it felt like you were just going on and on about things that happened so long ago. I'm a different person.

He doesn't want me to say the same things, even when he says the same things.

I tell him he is the most important person in my life. I say:

I feel totally confident about the longevity of our relationship and our intimacy and trust, but still I don't feel secure. Because of that five-year period when you lied about everything.

I say: That was the first conversation, because the last conversation I didn't say anything.

He says the first conversation, I say yeah the one from a month ago.

He says what do you mean you didn't say anything—is that how you remember the conversation, I just got angry and then left?

He's angry again. I don't say anything. I'm wondering if he's going to leave now, leave now and then this is the end. I'm wondering if I want him to leave.

THE BEACH

When I was twelve, I decided I couldn't wear glasses anymore. I wanted contacts, but my mother insisted that boys weren't supposed to be vain. I would drop my glasses off escalators, but they would just get dented. In school I held the frames in front of my eyes whenever I needed to read something on the blackboard. The teacher said: Isn't it more important to see?

I'd always liked teachers, except for the ones who didn't like me. But sometimes they said the stupidest things. Eventually I got contacts, but then I lost one—I didn't tell my parents because then we would have to fight about it. For a year I closed my left eye a lot. This was when my parents decided I needed therapy: I was refusing to wear the clothes they picked out for me. I didn't tell them anything. Most of my friends were girls.

My parents wanted me to see a therapist, so he would tell them what was going on. Since my parents were therapists, I knew this was unethical, but kids aren't part of ethics unless they do something wrong. I didn't want to be part of kids.

The first time I tried smoking was in the basement of my therapist's office, the same building as the pediatrician but you went through the front entrance like you were living in one of the apartments. I liked that part. I also liked the basement—it was a fallout shelter, which I never really understood: in the case of a nuclear war, could you really stay safe in a random basement with a cigarette machine and a brown corduroy sofa? I decided to try Benson & Hedges Menthol—the package looked the most sophisticated. I put the cigarette in my mouth: it tasted bitter, not minty like I'd expected but I lit it anyway and then inhaled through my nose.

I started coughing: smoking was awful. But I liked going into the laundry room, just because it was the laundry room in an apartment building. Sometimes I would walk back and forth from laundry room to fallout shelter—my therapist had a waiting room upstairs, but usually I arrived early and all he had in the waiting room was the *New Yorker*, which I thought was the most boring magazine ever created. At least my father's office had *Time* and *Newsweek*.

Maybe that's another thing I didn't like about the waiting room—it was kind of like waiting for my father. The therapist even had a beard, do all psychiatrists have beards? And the same furniture in his office: teak wood, brown hues. But his mother wasn't an artist like my grandmother, because I can't remember what was on his walls. I guess therapists are supposed to have unmemorable art, but I didn't think about that then—I just thought he had bad taste.

Twelve was when my parents sent us to sleepaway camp, that means my sister was ten. I was stuck in a cabin full of boys—each one taunted me in a different way. I wrote a letter to my parents every night: Please let me come home. Please. For three whole pages. I don't know what else I said, something about how the boys were bullying me and one of them broke my tennis racket but I didn't know how to get him to replace it. There used to be a whole shoebox full of letters in my father's office, but when I asked my mother to make copies the shoebox disappeared. Did they send us to camp for one month or two? At least one letter a day and sometimes, when I couldn't stop crying, the camp administrator let me call my parents but all they did was send more candy. Sour balls. Saltwater taffy. Lemon drops. Firecrackers. Bazooka bubble gum. Bubblicious. Chiclets. Juicy Fruit. Teaberry. Mike and Ikes. Necco Wafers. Now and Laters.

My mother was always on a diet, and my father was always taunting her. He would squeeze her thigh and say Karla, your legs are getting big. If she got annoyed, he would smile like she was a kid and say Karla, don't get agitated. My father looked at a photo of me at age two, framed in my grandmother's apartment, and said: Most fat babies grow up to be fat adults. I stopped eating.

One time I was in the car with my father on the way home from school, telling him about my day. He never listened anymore. He just said okay, that sounds good. So I said: I'm just going to get off right here and lie down in the middle of traffic. And he said okay, that sounds good.

Every dinner another battle, that time when my mother put a whole chicken on my plate: Oh, eat what you want. If they fought with heat, I needed to use cold, but if they feigned that casual tone then the only thing I could do was break it: I threw the whole chicken into the trash, rushing into my room while my father rushed after me, pounding on my door. He was always pounding on my door. Maybe this was Tracy Chapman time—I've got a fast car—tears in eyes through those not-quite-vertical blinds and hoping one of these days I'll drive drive drive away.

One of these days I do drive away. But then I drive back. We all drive back. But that's later, we haven't gotten to Tracy Chapman yet. Let's return to the dining room table, teak, this was when everyone in the family was obsessed with my weight. Maybe this was after we got back from Europe and my grandmother said: You look like a concentration camp victim.

I'd just seen glass display cases filled with human hair, but my grandmother's disapproval made me realize one thing: maybe I'm succeeding. I wanted to beat my father at his own game—when he became enraged, I would stare through him like there was something fascinating on the wall right behind his head: Bill, is there something wrong?

There was always something wrong, except at the dinner table when my father smiled and started laughing even before he spoke: Is that all you're going to eat? Then everyone else joined in: Is that all, is that all you're going to eat? I threw my plate onto the floor—really the floor? This must have been Tracy Chapman time.

Before I started drinking, I liked to say that I didn't need alcohol because I was so happy. Did anyone believe the act? I'm standing frozen in the camera's gaze, one shoulder up way higher than the other and I'm rail-thin, hair in an overgrown bowl cut and I guess the scary part is the way I'm standing, like in shock except this is a pose, a pose for the camera.

And then my eyes: like I've already left, this is my body I'm not here this is. Smile. Sometimes everyone knows what they can't see, and what they can see they don't know. Those first twelve years when I wore the exact same clothes as my father, bronze-rimmed eyeglasses literally the same shape as his, the only difference is that somehow I got away with wearing a women's watch with the skinnier band, my wrist was too small for the men's watch. Probably they didn't call it a women's watch, even if sometimes people would call me she. Adults: accidentally. Kids: on purpose.

Another picture from that same period, slightly earlier because my hair is shorter but they both say 6/85 on the back. I'm so glad pictures used to come with the date imprinted, it's helpful now. In the second picture I'm standing in the exact same position, the light even reflects off my glasses in the same way, rose almost—maybe it's the metal. This time I'm wearing a beige Izod shirt instead of the green one and it makes me look paler, like I'm going to fade into that shirt except for my chapped lips. My belt is wrapped high and tight around my waist like maybe I could get smaller. It makes the jeans hang strangely around the hips, extra fabric.

In the background, the *National Geographic World Atlas*: I'm memorizing all the world capitals. After the picture I'll go back to reading, or wrapping fingers around wrists—thumb to middle finger, thumb to ring finger, can I reach thumb to pinky? I worry about the skin I can squeeze, that means I'm getting fat. Especially in Hebrew school, where everyone calls me Mental and they don't mean it as a compliment. Sounds like my Hebrew name a river in Israel the same as my mother's dead father and I try to disappear into more words, letters shaped differently: I don't know what they mean, but I can sound them out more clearly than anyone else in the room and they hate me for it.

At first I was angry about therapy, another attempt by my parents to control my life, so I made up dreams: I talked about the beach and the way the water was always coming over the cliff I was holding onto. I didn't talk about how it was useful that my parents had so much liquor but they only drank beer. I started with Gilbey's gin from the basement—I thought since it was clear it wouldn't taste so awful but oh how it burned my throat, stomach, eyes. But then that amazing feeling in my head.

I brought that bottle of gin one time with me to Baltimore, after I discovered that Steve Pearls and I both liked to drink. Before that, we didn't have much to talk about: we were our fathers' sons and that was supposed to be enough. He liked baseball and looking for lizards in the alley and anything relating to science. The Pearls parents were both schoolteachers and there was a sandbox and swingset in their tiny backyard that wasn't really a yard because there wasn't any grass. The kids went to public school and their parents drove two beat-up Volkswagen Bugs, but usually one car wasn't working so they had to share. All the pillows in their house were flat. My father said they were middle class, and we were middle class, so I knew he was lying. He called me downstairs to his office and told me about the college accounts he'd created: $180,000 so far. He showed me where he kept the bank statements, don't tell your mother because then she'll want to spend it.

I remember sitting in my therapist's office, telling him of course I eat, if I didn't eat then how would I have all this energy? He said when you don't eat, sometimes that gives you energy. I discovered NoDoz, how else could I have survived high school? I cut the pills into parts so I didn't take too much at a time, that delicate rush. A few carrot sticks and maybe a bagel and a salad with no-cal dressing from the salad bar at Safeway, that would be enough for the day.

I learn to carry a hairbrush like a weapon, left front pocket, you never know when you might need it, rushing to the bathroom between periods to keep every hair in place. No longer the bowl cut, now I hold my hair up with mousse and spray. My hair glistens from the peroxide I comb in, soon I'll learn to look distant on purpose. First the skinny curler brush from Giant Foods with the fake wooden handle but later I move up to the one from the Body Shop with a green wooden recycled handle molded so your fingers fit one and then the next, a bigger curler brush with black bristles. This was high school, when people would say are you gay I would say everyone's bisexual.

But let's go back to sixth grade, that bathroom at recess where I could hear people playing outside, the smell of piss surrounding me—this was a separate building my school rented just for the sixth grade, so we were almost on our own. Behind the sports fields stood the Psychiatric Institute—that's where girls got sent for anorexia, came back tougher and sadder and more worldly. Sometimes I felt jealous.

This time I'm squinting because of the sun and my lips are turned to one side like I'm crying without crying. Then I'm in the same outfit, but on the New York subway, it's one of the trips when my father and I went to New York with Don and Steve Pearls. Here Don looks pensively into the distance, Steve gazes vaguely into the camera, and I look skittishly past my father, who's behind the camera. I loved the buildings, the taller the better—it didn't matter if my ears popped, as long as I could look down at everything. I loved walking out onto the street in front of the hotel and going into a corner store with all the hot food laid out on tables. We took the subway everywhere and I studied the neighborhoods—the end of the line was my favorite place, just because that meant we got to ride all the way back. Even better was an empty subway car from Coney Island where Steve and I would flow between the poles in the center, trying to stand up.

Before my bar mitzvah, I'd already rejected God, but on desperate nights I still prayed, face down into the pillow, before or after or maybe even during that grinding into the other pillow between my legs. My parents were the type that called themselves agnostic because they didn't want to risk the social exclusion of atheism. One Yom Kippur I told them I was fasting. My mother was worried I was going to become religious, for a moment this overrode her fears about my weight. Mostly my dreams were nightmares, except the ones that happened when I was awake, flying around with imaginary best friends in force-field bubbles and saving the kids who everyone refused to see.

I stopped wearing short-sleeved shirts: I didn't want anyone to see too much. At baseball games with my father and the Pearls, I keep score—then I can pretend everyone isn't looking at me like I don't belong. I don't belong. It's summer and I'm sweating, my father says it's because I'm not wearing short sleeves. I say why does it matter—I'd be sweating anyway.

My father loved to drink, but he loved control more, so he would only drink on Wednesdays and weekends. Sometime before our teenage years he started encouraging my sister and me to join in. I would stare at him with the disgust I was crafting—my sister would sip hungrily and my father would get excited. Boys' Night Out was different, that's when I used to love the cheesecake the best but now I tried to fit all my food into napkins I stuffed into the vinyl booths of the Jewish deli. Actually this was after Boys' Night Out became Kids' Night Out, which somehow meant dinner with my sister and my father, but where was my mother? She needed a break. My father would exaggerate his excitement at every bite of cheesecake— don't you want a bite, just one bite?

This is when the back pain starts, like my body is going to split apart right above my waist, no not when the back pain starts but when I start going to doctors for it. They tell me there's nothing wrong except a slight curve in my spine and we'll give you cookies for that—that's what they call the arch supports in my shoes. They don't help. I go to specialists. They send me to other specialists. I get a headache that never ends, no one knows what to do except ibuprofen, or stronger prescription drugs that are like ibuprofen but more colorful. I like the texture of the pills.

Puberty, a body—I wanted to keep pulling this belt tighter. I needed to count how many calories—it was so hard to get under 1,000, so hard when I would rush to the corner store after school, buy every candy bar I couldn't eat, take one bite of each and then throw the rest in the garbage. Afterwards I'd assess the damage: 1/10 of a Twix, 1/12 of a Milky Way, 3 Skittles—how many calories is that? Oh, no—there's another Skittle in my bag, should I eat it? At therapy I would say: Of course I eat, of course I eat because I have all this energy.

This energy in my head, I realized: No one will ever find me, if I can't show them something besides fear. I started dressing in clothes I thought might reflect something: first it was Generra sweatshirts, baggy Union Bay pants, Wayfarer sunglasses like Tom Cruise except now when I see pictures of Tom Cruise from that time he didn't wear those sunglasses, so who did? In seventh grade Gabe asked me to borrow my sweatshirt so he could look trendy. And I gave it right to him, before realizing he was making fun of me.

Gabe was one of the kids I admired, like Zelda Alpern when she bleached her hair with Clorox and it all fell out in the front—we'd been close friends in second and third grade and I still remembered her mother, who was always so friendly, and how we always had ginger snaps around at our house because Zelda was allergic to eggs. But in seventh grade she was dating

Gabe, one of the mod kids who listened to The Monkees and The Who before they realized mod wasn't tough enough so then they became punk.

I graduated to pegged jeans and V-neck sweaters over black turtlenecks, black loafers with dimes instead of pennies because I liked silver better: this was eighth grade. The mods who later became punks never paid much attention to me, even when I got a leather motorcycle jacket in New York—I just looked like more of a faggot, most of them never said that because they were too cool but still I knew it was a problem. Even in high school when I went to the smoking area, a small hill on the other side of the Safeway parking lot from our high school, they pretended not to see me.

I wanted people to think I was someone besides that kid who answered every question first, the one who sat down for second-grade reading group and finished everything in the whole series through the eighth-grade level, the end of the series. This was the kind of school where everyone remembered that kind of thing, but in high school there were all these new kids who didn't belong. Soon they belonged and I still didn't. I realized I would never belong, and I didn't want to belong with these people anyway. That's when I figured out how I would find people.

Back to 1977: I'm four and my sister's two. We're sitting on the floor of our new house, and in front of us on the rug is a pile of Legos. I'm smiling huge, and my sister looks like she's been caught by the camera—she's just knocked over the Legos and her mouth is in between expressions. In the second picture I'm leaning down toward the Legos, and my sister has her arm around me. Take these Legos, I want to say—we can take these Legos and build a house where they can't find us. My sister knocks it over, and then we smile, smile for the camera. Soon we'll leave this house, my parents want something bigger, we're moving up.

This was the thing with our family: we were always moving up, but somehow we always stayed middle class. Actually, we weren't just middle class, things were tight—that's what my father kept repeating. If my mother spent too much at Bloomingdale's, or I got too many bottles of Evian, there might not be enough for college.

My father fetishized these types of habits: burping at the table, farting and talking about it, pissing with the door open to the bathroom, eating with loud slurping sounds, smacking his lips—manners were for others, others who weren't struggling like he was, that's what he wanted us to believe. One time we were at the dinner table with the whole extended family, a rare occasion, in my mind it's that same time I threw my plate of food to the floor, but it couldn't have been the same time, could it? Anyway, we were all getting ready for dinner and my father said to my mother: Karla, let's fuck. My mother looked stunned—Bill, you've got to be kidding. They went into their room and locked the door, we waited for dinner.

But let's go back to the Pearls—Don was my father's childhood friend, the only one we ever heard about. We would see the Pearls about once a month—my father and I would go down for baseball games, and then we started going to indoor soccer in the fall and my sister liked soccer so she and my mother came too but my mother didn't like it so she didn't come very often. The Pearls would join us every year at the beach for a week of our two-week vacation, and my father and I would go with Steve and Don to New York once a year. The whole family would come over our house for New Year's when my parents would have parties. There was something that didn't click between my mother and Anne, something about how my parents were raising us: Anne didn't understand how we were allowed to talk back.

But back to puberty, a body I didn't want, that time when I was ready to say something, something other than what they wanted. I wanted contact lenses. This was when I went to the doctor, they were worried about my weight: 81 pounds. The doctor looked at a chart—80 to 120 pounds was normal for my age.

A victory and a defeat: I wanted to get under 80 pounds, but it's hard to lose weight when everything is changing, you were tall before but now you're six inches taller. I understood this, I understood it meant I would never win. But I looked at Dan Abraham one time when we were changing for PE, and I saw all this extra flesh on his body. We weren't friends anymore, now that we had bodies. Muscle was the same as fat to me and he was an athlete, always good at sports and I was so glad to see that extra flesh at his belly when he bent over, something I didn't have. I went back to writing down calories: 3 rice cakes, 37 calories each; 10 carrot sticks, 30 calories total; a bagel, 160 calories; an apple, was that a large or small apple?

There are double doors, double doors to my father's office. So his patients don't hear his other patients. In my psychiatrist's office, there are double doors too—one of them swings open and blocks the view from the waiting room: maybe there are no other patients. There is a time when my father says to me: You could put dead bodies in a mulch pile and no one would know. We have a mulch pile in the backyard, the backyard of our new house, and this is when I'm floating. There is a time when my father says: You can inject drugs into someone's head and no one would know. My father the doctor, the doctor with drugs. There is my head, my head and my father's eyes and there is no one, no one would know.

When I was little it was always hard to go to the bathroom. It was scary because it hurt so much, there was blood and there was shit and there were worms and the doctor always said wash your hands. There was never a time when I didn't wash my hands and I always had worms and the doctor would say don't forget, don't forget to wash your hands. The way the room would become everything except, nothing but my father's eyes and this pain, down there this pain and the smell in my mouth his fingers opening closing my mouth I can't. I can't. His, his, down there, that pain and the smell and there is a broken toy and I will never know.

Sometimes my mother forgets to bring a washcloth, she yells to me from the bathroom to ask for one and then when I get there she's standing naked, there's the smell of something metallic in the room, my father's hair caked to the floor from shaving and that smell and I am a broken toy. I know about the Velveteen Rabbit, the skin horse that says what is real?

In second grade, my teacher called a conference with my parents. She was worried that all my friends were girls. Like Jeannine LeFlore, who lost her ring in school one day and she was crying and we all searched the whole classroom until eventually I found the ring, it was on a shelf in the corner. Was that before or after I hid my grandmother's keys and sometimes jewelry?

Another conversation with my father in his office, maybe I'm fourteen. I say: You're not middle class, you're rich. He starts screaming. I stand there so calm it's unbelievable, or not calm but quiet, cold, I'm fighting to win. The Pearls are middle class, I say—they have two broken-down cars, they own their house, they shop at discount stores, and they struggle to pay the bills.

Eventually my father backs down: Okay, we're upper-middle class.

But before this conversation, I start cooking my own food. I don't think my mother should have to cook everything. And if I cook then I can make sure there's no fat, no fat on my boneless breast of Dijon chicken with the calories labeled on back. My mother isn't a good cook anyway. I start doing my own dishes—everyone should do their own dishes. I do my own laundry, and shut my door so the housekeeper doesn't have to clean my room but then she always goes in anyway because my mother opens the door.

I go into my room and there my mother is, sitting at my desk, reading my journal. What are you doing in my room? I'm reading, I like the light in here, I'll get out of your way.

Here's my sister in 1984, squinting in the wind on the beach and she's listening to something on her Walkman, she's nine but she's already a teenager. No, wait—I'm nine—my sister's seven, but she's already a teenager. Here's my mother, separately, smiling for the camera and she looks angry.

I want to tell you about the beach, if I keep digging in the sand then eventually I'll get to China. Sometimes I reach water: I'm almost there. The best part is when Steve arrives, and then I can go deeper into the ocean without my father nearby. My favorite thing is to jump up into a wave and float over the top, but Steve likes to go under. I'm worried about choking from all that salt in my mouth, but then eventually we both end up getting pummeled anyway, sand coating the insides of our bathing suits that later we'll have to turn inside-out. Or the undertow pulls us in too far and Anne Pearls gets worried—no one else is paying attention. The only way to get back is to let a wave hit you. Steve likes getting knocked over, but sometimes, rolling around underwater my head into the sand I get scared like maybe I'll be buried with the sand crabs and someone will have to dig me out.

The good thing about the sand crabs is that they go right

back under. They're so fast. And the tiny little baby clams, you can watch them pushing water away to get back underneath. There's so much to watch, as long as those flies with the red eyes aren't all over the place like right after a storm, when there are huge horseshoe crabs littering the beach and even stranded sting rays. Sometimes the horseshoe crabs are still trying to live—it's sad. In the water after a storm, there are too many jellyfish, you have to keep dodging them—even if it's raining, I want to be in the water.

This is the Sea Colony, really a colony the way they built eight nine-story condo towers right on the beach, in this tiny town that barely even has a boardwalk, not like Ocean City with huge glittering towers or Rehoboth with crowds and rides. This colony stretches across the street which is really a highway, where there are whole neighborhoods with different names, and lakes and tennis courts. There's always a new development—on the other side you can get a whole house for cheaper than a condo on this side, but my parents chose this side because of the beach. We can go on our balcony, and right outside, past the elevated cement walkway that goes from one building to the next, there's nothing but the ocean. It's fun to sit at the glass table with the chairs you can sit on when you're still wet and just listen, listen to the ocean.

It's better when the Pearls are there, then my parents don't argue as much. Even my sister is quieter, and then there's so much time to float in the ocean. Sometimes I try to swim out as far as possible, just to see if there are any islands. Who is that girl in this one picture, 1985, digging in the sand? It's true that girls could go shirtless until a certain age, but she looks older, building an enormous hill in the sand oh wait it's shaped like a heart. It kind of looks like Cindy Pearls, but I don't remember Cindy digging in the sand much.

When do we start going out by ourselves, the four kids, just us? Walk into Bethany for miniature golf and peppermint ice cream, salt water taffy, the video arcade with the local kids who wear all black and smoke a lot and don't talk to us. Except when one of them leans over while I'm getting the high score on Galaga, so he can say: Are you a boy or a girl? One of my favorite things about the Pearls: no one ever asks me that.

Steve tries to act like a parent because he's the oldest but Allison won't take any of it. I try to help Cindy not to feel bullied. We do this at home too, like the time when we go to a Chinese restaurant on the Rockville Pike, right near the video rental place, and we have our own table. There's a show on the restaurant TV about ice, the new designer drug, and Steve says he saw it once. Does it really look like ice?

We lived in Rockville but went to school in the city, so we never knew any of our neighbors except the ones next door and that was only because we played with their dog. Rockville was subdivisions where all the houses looked the same, but in our neighborhood every house was different and the yards were bigger, kind of like Potomac, the wealthiest neighborhood in the DC suburbs, at least on the Maryland side, and since our neighborhood was even called Potomac Highlands, Potomac sounded better. Our mail would get sent back if we wrote Potomac 20854, but most of the time it worked out if we wrote Potomac 20850, which was the Rockville zip code, so that's where we decided we lived: Potomac 20850, all by ourselves. Actually I decided that, and then everyone went along. What privilege did for me: it kept me there. I was my parents' biggest investment, they needed me to stay invested.

Sometimes we would drive around—DC, Maryland, Delaware—we would drive around, looking at houses. I would imagine a house where there weren't problems, maybe something bigger or more modern, like the new development down the street from us, the one that wasn't really a development because there were only six houses and they were all different, contemporary, with big glass windows and sharp angles. Even better would be one of the mansions on Embassy Row, where I could have my own entrance. Or a high-rise, then it didn't matter where it was as long as I could live in my own apartment on the top floor.

But first I wanted it to be us against them, me and my sister, us against the world of our parents. We could create our own world, a world where we could keep things for each other, secrets. My sister would get enraged like my father, every secret a weapon until I knew I could never trust. If I stopped breathing then I'd never need. I can't remember a single one of those secrets anymore, it was so hard to forget.

This arguing they said meant they loved each other, my mother was always threatening to leave him; I wanted that too then maybe something would be okay. I read all the Hardy Boys, the Nancy Drews when no one was looking, the Hornblower books, *Watership Down* in third grade because it was the longest book at the school book fair, all the Agatha Christie's by the end of fifth and when there was no more mystery I moved on to the classics: *War and Peace* and *Crime and Punishment* in sixth grade. My teacher was worried I was missing out on childhood, she wanted my mother to read to me.

I remember when my sister read *Are You There God? It's Me, Margaret* and she started practicing the moves: all the girls did it, even if you didn't believe. Like the boys who taunted me, shaking chest and pelvis and screeching I must, I must, I must increase my bust—they were telling me I was worse than those girls repeating Judy Blume's words over and over, because all I could do was want. Like praying to God at night, into the pillow, before or during or after I would grind into the mattress to that dark place where I would dream of being smothered to death in shit, this was desire.

Puberty, a body, this worked out better for my sister. I wanted to play with dolls and wear frilly sweaters and paint my room pink. I wanted to wear tights with cutoff shorts. I wanted dresses and makeup and moisturizer. I wanted to giggle and gossip and talk about boys and boobs and ask my friends if I looked fat. I wanted to eat nothing but carrot sticks and rice cakes and salads with no-cal dressing and watch adults smile at me and think my diet was cute.

Sometimes I'd sit on my sister's bed and try to imagine what it would be like if I were underneath the covers, would things be easier? She would scream and yell and tell my secrets and I would hope for the calm moments when we could dream together.

There were no secrets in my journal, the one my sister and my mother read. Other secrets I remember, the ones I would never tell, like that first time in the bathroom at Woodie's. Now Woodie's sounds like a gay bar and not the department store on the way to my father's office, but I didn't know about gay bars yet. I knew there were restaurants in Rehoboth Beach—The Back Porch, The Blue Moon, La La Land—my parents went there for the food, the atmosphere, but we weren't allowed, my father said there were too many fairies.

Oh, that bottle of Gilbey's gin, that feeling in my head, the stomachache. New Year's with the Pearls became so much more fun, except for the vomit behind my bed. My sister and I would lock the doors to our rooms and we'd all run back and forth to tell each other something. The four of us started drinking around the same time—Allison and Cindy were younger but succeeding at becoming popular in a way that would never work for me or Steve, but for different reasons. I didn't under-stand his reasons exactly, but maybe that's why we got along: we didn't ask. And there was that bottle of Gilbey's gin—or let's not be silly there were other bottles now—luckily there were two liquor cabinets in the house, one downstairs behind the built-in bar where my parents had an elaborate party when we first moved in, over 100 guests, but after the party they never looked behind the bar again, except. Except my father's eyes and that smell of mold in the bathroom sink, hand me that Gilbey's gin again.

I remember when my sister and I watched *Less Than Zero* with the Pearls—maybe I hadn't even tried pot yet, but I watched Robert Downey Jr. shake from line after line of all that pure white pure white until he was in a car smoking from a glass pipe and oh I wanted to be that light on Robert Downey Jr's face. This is when I didn't want to be perfect anymore, I didn't want to keep anything or anyone together that shouldn't be together. At therapy, I would talk about how trapped I felt, doomed, maybe just like Robert Downey Jr. at the end of the movie when someone scrawls FAGGOT on the wall of his house or some bungalow where he's slept with some guy for more coke, way after graduation with all the champagne and palm trees and mirrored bathrooms and runny noses and tearful hello-goodbyes. I thought it was in Florida, but it must've been Southern California—growing up in DC they seemed like the same thing: it was hot, there were palm trees, people wore bathing suits. But I didn't say any of that. I just said I felt trapped.

My father would say: That waitress was stacked, that wait-ress was stacked like a brick shithouse. Loudly. At the restau-rant. To my mother, who would smile: Oh, Bill! He thought that if he said things like that often enough, in between writing papers about borderline personality disorder, maybe that would make him working class. He published his first book and everyone was very proud, especially his mother, the artist, the artist who liked to tell a story about when my father wanted to become a writer, before or after college I'm not sure but she said to him: Okay, then you pay all the bills. He went to medical school.

There was one thing my father and I agreed on: rich meant evil. The good news was that a $360 sweater would eventually go on sale for $36, and I figured out I could make that happen faster if I changed the labels. Still I wanted to make sure each outfit added up to at least $100, even though I didn't want anyone to know it had cost more than Value Village. Maybe this was like counting calories, only the reverse.

It was hard for me to get to the makeup counter, I didn't know what to say: I'm looking for a base to cover up my acne, I mean my mother's acne? I was on the way from school to my father's office, I would wait for him until he was done with his patients, and then he would drive me home. I stopped at Woodie's to look for that base, but I was too scared to talk to the person at the makeup counter. So I ended up buying Evian water in a metal can, with a nozzle so you could spray a delicate mist over your face. Actually in the DC humidity it was wonderful, did I have the Woodie's credit card yet? No one used that one much, it wasn't upscale enough but now they were renovating.

But then the bathroom, black tile and I'm standing at the urinal because that's what my father says I'm supposed to do, even though it's hard not to get too nervous that someone will think I'm looking. There it is, reflected in the black tile, this guy next to me, he drops his hand. I can't breathe. I drop my hand too, he's looking. I reach for his dick and it's spongy, warm;

he reaches for mine and we stand there like that for maybe thirty seconds or three minutes or three years. There's no way to know anything except I can't breathe and this warmth in my hand and then someone comes in and I pull back quickly, stuff it into my pants, walk as fast as I can without looking like I'm running, out the back door, down the hill and up the block to my father's office.

First there was the end of everything, and then there was childhood, a trap, and then there was that place between childhood and the world. Here I am at twelve again, standing in a field. I'm wearing the same colors as the scenery, my hair reddish in the setting sun with the reddening leaves of the trees, green shirt blending into the evergreens, navy pants between the mountains and sky. When did my father and I start those bike rides—another opportunity for him to scream at me, scream because I was going too slow over bridges I was worried I would fall off. Scream at me when he was trying to teach me to throw, to throw like a boy. This was baseball, the first sport I was required to take but it didn't work out because I was afraid of the ball when they threw it in my direction.

Here's the entrance to our bike ride: a small parking lot. There's always a Mercedes parked here, the same Mercedes, an old sedan in that color somewhere between green and brown, a color so ugly to me that I imagined it could only mean you knew you could never fail. Except then it's actually for sale, for sale at a low price and I try to convince my father.

The park, there must have been something pretty about the park: I just remember trying not to fly off bridges. Maybe the trees, the trees and the light, the trees and the light and the air yes sometimes the air when we went fast or slow and he wasn't yelling at me, yelling at me for something, nothing and one time I fell and hit my head and we went to the hospital and I needed stitches and after that I wore a helmet, we wore helmets, and then there wasn't any air anymore.

The next sport was basketball, they said I was tall I would be good at basketball. I couldn't understand the connection between my body in this room the ball in my fingertips and legs. We settled on soccer, no we didn't settle they just left me there on that hill in all that sun and loneliness. Soccer was better because I could kick the ball and then everyone would go away for a few minutes.

Somehow I got to the makeup counter again, I was looking for a suitable base for my mother, she had the same skin color as me—oh, we could test it out on my wrist, what a good idea. Maybe a cover-up for under the eyes too, how does that work exactly? And an eye cream for the bags under my eyes, I mean my mother's eyes. A powder, what kind of powder would be best? By the time of that first bathroom it was karate, the sport I was required to take, at least with karate you were on your own. And they had these dance moves they called forms, where you twirled around to Beethoven.

Wait—remember that picture of the girl building a heart-shaped sand castle? I look closer: that's not Cindy Pearls, it's me.

But back to my parents, secrets between children and the threat, the threat we posed. The biggest threat to the biggest secret is another secret. We didn't even know there was something to tell, even though there is an end there is no end.

Never again I would say after every visit to the bathroom at Woodie's, or Mazza Gallery across the street, the mall fancy enough to think of itself as art, where I really wanted those Gaultier sunglasses with the blue lenses, but they were more expensive than my sweaters and there were no tags to change. Every day after school, even though I would always say never again. They would look at me with so much hunger, these men, old men mostly, older than my father and paler too, so many of them would get sweat-drenched and pink and I would try not to feel it, what was happening between my legs.

I didn't call it sex, not even to myself. I knew that if I ever mentioned it then no one would ever let me be anything else. I would practice standing with my hands in my pockets and my knees slightly bent, head cocked up oh that's this pose in the picture in front of a tiled wall in 1987, where I almost succeed at looking tough for the camera there was always someone watching. Here's one from later, undated, I think it's later because my face has lengthened and I've moved on from that earlier pose into the same pose but more defiant. I'm telling the camera: you don't matter. Nothing matters. I can see this kid in those bathrooms, I can see what they were seeing in this kid.

But let's go back to that bottle of Gilbey's gin, we already know that bottle is long gone and now I like vodka better anyway—my sister prefers the darker liquors so it works out okay, this one might be Gilbey's vodka. This is Baltimore, after Steve and I have realized we both drink but before the four of us start climbing out windows at the beach so we can go downstairs with the other kids to drink late at night, the kids who start to look up to me because I'm not worried when my sister runs off with some random boy. I'm reading Sartre and I believe in freedom. They don't know what I'm reading, they just think I'm weird. Maybe not too weird. This is when the beach really matters.

But before the beach, there's Baltimore and that bottle yes that bottle I'm with Steve and three of his friends, guys from the neighborhood. We're in the drug-free school zone while our fathers are touring the Irish bars, they like the dark beers with a lot of head, that's what my father says.

There is so much joy, so much joy in this bottle. Everyone else is drinking beer and that makes me tougher so I hold the bottle out for anyone who dares. This is when no one knows and no one cares and I'm just everything that matters exploding into the world. And we're on a hill looking down but also looking up because that's what this bottle means and there's so much love, that's what I'm feeling. I've never been allowed to feel this love and we're laughing, laughing when we're not sucking on cigarettes we need more cigarettes on this hill looking down we start walking. I take the bottle in my mouth, the rest of that burning joy to my head I shake in the way you have to and my eyes, now we're in an empty parking lot. I take that bottle I hurl it straight up into the air as far as I can get it, underhand like I'm not supposed to but I don't think about that I don't think about anything except the sky.

ACKNOWLEDGMENTS

To the wonderful critics and friends, friends and critics who gave me detailed analysis of the manuscript in various forms: Katia Noyes, Jory Mickelson, Jennifer Natalya Fink, D. Travers Scott, Sarah Schulman and Laurie Sirois.

For thoughtful feedback on several key moments: Gina Carducci, Andy Slaght, Socket Klatzker, Eric Stanley, Lauren Goldstein, Ralowe T. Ampu, Johanna Fateman.

For tangibles and intangibles: Kevin Coleman, Jessica Lawless, Jessica Hoffmann, Dana Garza, Yasmin Nair, Meghan Storms, Marisa Hackett, Alex West, Kirk Read, Magdalena Ward, Scott Philips, Carrie Philips, Erik Eyster, Ellen Yu, Zee Boudreaux, Eve Stotland, Eric von Stein, Steve Zeeland, Ananda La Vita, Keith Hennessy, Stephen Kent Jusick, Tim Doody, Clio Reese Sady, Kara Davis, Jane McAndrew, Elizabeth Norman, Korn, Jennifer Flynn, Staci Smith, Bill Dobbs, Dean Spade, Craig Willse, Kathryn Welsh, Karen Sundheim, Justin Torres, Jim Van Buskirk, Daphne Gottlieb, Reginald Lamar, Kevin Killian, Jen Cross, Michael Bronski, Hedi El Kholti, Daria Yudacufski, Daniel Allen Cox, Jason Sellards, T Cooper, Gina de Vries, Michelle Tea, Michael Lowenthal, Gabriel Hedemann, Jon Curley, Erica Berman, Hilary Goldberg, Rhani Remedes, Sugar Magnolia Edwards, Charlie Stephens, Cary Cronenwett, Chris Mielen, Billay Tania, Camelia Perlis, Hank Gaypuff, blake nemec, Seeley Quest, Wheels Darling, Von Edwards, Jess Clark, Justin Ray, c.d. wright, Elisa Glick, Donna Bervinchak, Sheri Cohen, Jeff Thompson, Glenn Lee, Jackie Carrera, Dennis Casey, Scott Berry, Rebecca Shuman, Thea Hillman, Elizabeth Stark, and all the queens who taught me how to walk. And walk. And walk. And anyone else who I may have inadvertently forgotten—in spite of the length of this list, I'm sure there are many.

And even my mother, who said: "It feels like I'm right there with you, like I'm not looking at it from a distance—almost like a movie but it's not fantasy it's real."

Can I even thank Chris Hammett, the friend who let me down the most? What happens to before, after?

To all the activists I've organized with—in ACT UP, Fed Up Queers, and Gay Shame, as well as all the other named and unnamed groups.

For publishing excerpts of this book, in various forms: *Chroma, The Political Edge* (edited by Chris Carlsson), *Make/shift, Maximum Rock 'n' Roll, Eleven Eleven.*

There are editors, and then there are editors. And then there is Elaine Katzenberger, my editor at City Lights, who studied the manuscript meticulously, who said to me at one point that she couldn't sleep the night before, in part because she was thinking about a particular chapter, going over the structure in her head, trying to figure out what would work best! And to Stacey Lewis, my publicist, who supported this project even before it was signed. To everyone at City Lights— this is truly a City Lights book, and I am so grateful for it.

ABOUT THE AUTHOR

Described as "a cross between Tinkerbell and a honky Malcolm X with a queer agenda" by the *Austin Chronicle* and one of "50 Visionaries Changing Your World" by *Utne Reader*, Mattilda Bernstein Sycamore is the author of two novels, *So Many Ways to Sleep Badly* and *Pulling Taffy*, and the editor of five nonfiction anthologies, most recently *Why Are Faggots So Afraid of Faggots? Flaming Challenges to Masculinity, Objectification, and the Desire to Conform*. Sycamore is also the editor of *Nobody Passes: Rejecting the Rules of Gender and Conformity* and *That's Revolting! Queer Strategies for Resisting Assimilation*. She writes regularly for a variety of publications, including the *San Francisco Bay Guardian*, *Bitch*, *Bookslut*, *Alternet*, and *Time Out New York*, and is the reviews editor at the feminist magazine *Make/shift*. She is currently at work on a third novel, *Sketchstasy*. Visit mattildabernsteinsycamore.com.

1/6/15